Caroline County, Virginia

Order Book

1764

Ruth and Sam Sparacio

HERITAGE BOOKS
2020

HERITAGE BOOKS
AN IMPRINT OF HERITAGE BOOKS, INC.

Books, CDs, and more—Worldwide

For our listing of thousands of titles see our website
at
www.HeritageBooks.com

Published 2020 by
HERITAGE BOOKS, INC.
Publishing Division
5810 Ruatan Street
Berwyn Heights, Md. 20740

International Standard Book Number
Paperbound: 978-1-68034-553-7

CAROLINE COUNTY, VIRGINIA
ORDER BOOK
1764-1765

(This Book begins with a page numbered 51. It is partially torn and undated)

.... the repairs to the Prison & make report

.... the Court proceeded to finish the County Levy. Brought forward 17261 lbs of Tobacco. Secretary p account 744. WILLIAM CAMPBELL and JOHN HOOMES for clearing a Road near Todd 10/each; to WILLIAM HARRISON on Account DAVID GORDON a Criminal; to Do for taking care of the Stables etc; to BENJAMIN BOUGHAN for apprehending & take care of a criminal Slave; to PEYTON STERN per account for repairing the Prison; to the Sheriff for collecting the above 19137 lbs of Tobo. Debit; by 163 lbs of Tobo in JOHN SUTTONs hands as late Sheriff which he agreed to account for in Money at fourteen shillings per hundred including the difference of two shillings per hundred on the four thousand pounds Tobo Sold last year as also including a balance in money of seventeen pounds & six shillings & one penny due from the sd SUTTON to the County; by 4628 Tithables @ 6 lbs Tobo per Poll

It is ordered the Sheriff receive for every Tithable person in this County 6 lbs Tobo & pay the same to the several persons levyed for

JANE QUARLES came into Court & made choice of ROGER QUARLES as her Guardian which was approved of by the Court who acknowledged a Bond for the same & ordered to be recorded

JOHN CHANDLERs Inventory is returned & admitted to record

The Division of the Estate of JAMES GOUCH Deced is returned & admitted to record

Page 52. February Court 1764.

(this page also partially torn.) The Division of GEORGE MARSHs Estate (torn) and admitted to record

A Deed from ROBERT LOWREY to WILLIAM (missing) further proved by the Oath of WILLIAM TURNER (torn) Witnesses thereto & admitted to record

It appearing necessary to the Court to have a Treasurer (torn) appointed to receive such sums as may be in the Sheriffs hand belonging to the County made choice of JAMES TAYLOR Gent & its ordered that he receive of JOHN SUTTON Gent late high Sheriff the sum of one hundred & thirty five pounds Six shillings & a pence current money for the use of this County

Ordered that the Treasurer pay JOHN TAYLOR Gent nineteen pounds for Books for the use of the County

It appearing to the Court that WM. UBANK is not capable of taking care of his children, Its ordered that the Churchwardens of St. MARGARETs PARISH do bind WILLIAM UBANK JUNR. to EUCLID WHITLOCK & bind the other Children out according to Law

EDMOND PENDLETON & JOHN TAYLOR Gentl.
Exors of JAMES TAYLOR Deceased Plaintiffs v
WILLIAM BOWLER Deft. The former order in this Suit & the Gent formerly appointed Auditors to settle all matters in dispute are to proceed if either Plaintiff or Defendant fail to attend on having legal Notice

JAMES FARISHes Mortgage to THOMAS COLEMAN was proved by the oaths of the Witnesses & admitted to record

Page 53. February Court 1764

Ordered WILLIAM TYLER Gent CHRISTOPHER TOMPKINS, ROGER QUARLES & JOHN MINOR or any two do settle the Executorship of CARR McGEE of JOHN COMANs Estate & lay of the Widow her Dower

On the motion of WILLIAM POE & THOMAS REYNOLDS Securitys of ELIZABETH CHARLES for the administration of all & singular the goods and chattles Rights & Credits of OLIVER CHARLES deced be summoned to next Court to give them Counter Security

SAMUEL REDD, THOMAS LOWRY & JOHN MILLER JUNR. produced Commissions from under the Hand & Seale of his Honour the Governour to be Captains in this County who took Oaths appointed by Act of Parliament Read & Subscribed the Test

JOHN BROADDUS, JOHN CLARK, RICHARD ALLCOCK produced Commissions from under the hand & Seal of his Honour the Governour to be Lieutenants who took the Oaths appointed to be taken by Act of Parliament Read & Subscribed the Test

JOHN THOMPSON produced a Commission from his Honour the Governour to be Ensign who took the Oaths appointed to be taken by Act of Parliament read & subscribed the Test

A Mortgage from under the hand & Seal of JOHN WYNAL SAUNDERS to LARKIN CHEW was proved by the Oath of OLIVER TOWLES & ordered to be recorded

On the Petition of THOMAS REYNOLDS Its Ordered that ELIAS BLACKBURN, THOMAS CROUCHER, WILLIAM HOWARD, THOMAS SEALE or any three of them view the Roads from ELIAS BLACKBURNs to DICKIEs Quarter & make their report to the next Court

It is Ordered JAMES GATEWOOD, EUSIBIOUS STONE, BENJAMIN GATEWOOD, RICHARD EDMONDSON & JOHN WALDIN with the Gang under them, do clear the Road from BUCKS BRIDGE to (blurred) Creek & make the Bridge over the sd Creek that THOMAS DUDLEY, JOHN SNEED JUNR. & WILLIAM MOTLEY with their Ganges is to

Page 54 February Court 1764

open the Roads to the THREE NOTCHED ROAD by Mrs. FORSTERs and ROBERT CHOWNINGs, JAMES JAMESON Gent and Mrs. FORSTER agreeing the Roads shall go as first viewed nothwithstanding the Order for a review

An Indenture of Apprenticeship from LEWIS BULLARD to WILLIAM OWEN was approved of by the Court & admitted to Record

Then the Court adjourned till the Court in Course EDMD. PENDLETON

At a Court held for Caroline County on Munday the 14th day of February 1764 for the Examination of JOSEPH BATES

Present EDMD. PENDLETON, ROBERT GILCHRIST)
JAMES JAMESON, JAMES TAYLOR,) Gent Justices
WILLIAM PARKER & JOHN TAYLOR

JOSEPH BATES being committed to the Goal of this County by a Mittimus from under the hand & Seal of WILLIAM PARKER Gent one of his Majesties Justices of the Peace for the sd County on suspicion of Robing & breaking open the Storehouses of JOHN McDOUALL Merchant in HANOVER and being brought before this Court for examination pleaded not guilty on hearing & examining the Prisoner & the Witnesses against him, It is the Opinion of the Court that the Facts against the Prisoner are so sufficiently proved as that he ought thereupon to have a further tryal before the Judges of the next General

Court, It is Therefore Ordered that the sd JOSEPH BATES be remanded to the Goal of this County & the Sheriff of the sd County as soon as conveniently may be convey the prisoner to the publick Goal of this Colony in the

Page 55. February Court 1764

City of WILLIAMSBURG in order to have his further tryal before the Judges of the General Court.

HUGH McMACON, WILLIAM SOUTHWORTH and WILLIAM YOUNG severally acknowledged themselves & each of their Heirs to be bound unto our Sovereign Lord KING GEORGE his Heirs & Successors in the sum of Fifty pounds each to be levied on each of their goods, chattles, Lands & Tenements. THE CONDITION of the above Recognizance is such that if the above bound HUGH McMACON, WILLIAM SOUTHWORTH & WILLIAM YOUNG shall respectively be and appear at the next General Court to be held at the Capitol in the City of Williamsburg on the Sixth day thereof in order to give their Testimony in behalf of our Sovereign Lord KING GEORGE the Third & JOSEPH BATES the Prisoner & shall there remain till the (blurred) by the sd Court then the above Recognizance to be void or else to remain in full force & virtue

EDMD. PENDLETON

Page 56. Caroline County Court 8 March 1764

At a Court of Oyer and Terminer held at the Court house of Caroline County the eighth day of March 1764 on tryal of Tom a negro man Slave belonging to HENRY GILBERT of HANOVER COUNTY for felony and Burgalary

Present	EDMUND PENDLETON	ROBERT GILCHRIST	
	ANTHONY THORNTON	JAMES TAYLOR	Gent Justices
	WILLIAM PARKER	JOHN TAYLOR &	
		JOHN BAYNHAM	

Tom a Negro man Slave belonging to HENRY GILBERT of the County of HANOVER being committed to the Goal of this County by a Mittimus from under the hand and Seal of JOHN BAYNHAM Gent one of his Majesties Justices of the peace for the said County for felony and upon his arrignment pleaded not guilty. The Court proceeded to examine the witnesses against him Whereupon it is the opinion of the Court that he is guilty of the felony and Burghlary in the indictmt. mentioned and its ordered that he go from this place to the prison of the said County and from thence to the place of Execution and thereto be hanged by the neck till he be dead

Tom is valued at one hundred pounds which is ordered to be certified to the next Assembly.

EDMUND PENDLETON

Page 57. Caroline County Court 8 March 1764

At a Court held for Caroline County on Thursday the Eight Day of March 1764
Present: EDMUND PENDLETON, ANTHONY THORNTON,
JAMES TAYLOR & WILLIAM PARKER Gent. Justices

On the Motion of GEORGE TOD his Ordinary Licence is renewed who with ROBERT ARMISTEAD his Security acknowledged their Bond for the same

On the Petion of WILLIAM GRAVES his Ordinary Licence is renewed who with DAVID STERN his Security acknowledged their Bond for the same

DYNER DYER the Wife of JOHN DYER being first privately Examined relinquished her right of Dower of Lands sold by her Husband, JOHN DYER, to JAMES SPEARMAN

On the Petion of FRANCIS COLEMAN his Ordinary Licence is renewed who with WILLIAM GRAVES his Security acknowledged their Bond for the same

A Deed from JOHN DYER, DINAH DYER his Wife and ELISHA DYER Indented to DILLARD HARRIS was acknowledged by the said JOHN & DINAH his Wife the sd DINAH being first privately Examined and proved as to the sd ELISHA DYER by the Oath of three witnesses and admitted to record

On the Petion of WILLIAM PARKER Gent his Ordinary Licence is renewed who with JOHN PENN his Security acknowledged their bond for the same

The Indenture of apprenticeship from JAMES RYMES to JOSEPH DEJARNETT being first approved of by the Court was admitted to record

Page 57a. Caroline County Court 8 March 1764

A Deed indented from JOHN ASHBURN JUNR. to GARLAND ANDERSON was proved by the Oath of the Witnesses and admitted to Record

ROBERT WARDROPE Plt v BENJAMIN HOBBS Deft In Debt

Now at this day came GEORGE MAJOR who having at a Court held for this sd County in March 1763 undertook that in case the sd BENJAMIN HOBBS should be cast in the afore-sd Suit he would satisfie and pay the condemnation of the Court or render his Body to Prison in Execution of the same or that he the sd GEORGE MAJOR would do it for him Whereupon the sd GEORGE MAJOR did on the eight day of March deliver up the sd BENJAMIN to the sd Plt. in discharge of his undertaking aforesd and the sd Plaint. by his Atto. craved him in Execution which was granted him

THOMAS SULLINGER acknowledged his Deed Indented to THOMAS LENDRUM which was ordered to be recorded

JAMES BOWIE petitioning for Administration of ROBERT CALL deceased Estate & making Oath according to Law Certificate is granted him for obtaining Letters of Administration on the sd Estate in due form the sd JAMES together with ALEXANDER ROSE acknowledged their Bond for the same

The Settlement of JOHN COMERS Estate is returned & admitted to record

JOHN BAIRD etc. Plts. v FRANCIS COLEMAN Deft. In Case

By consent ofthe Parties the suit is referred to EDMUND PENDLETON and JOHN BAYLOR Gent their award to be the Judgment of this Court

Page 58. Caroline County Court 8 March 1764

RICHARD BUCKNER Plt. v WILLIAM BOWLER et al Defts. On Motion

This day came the sd Plaintiff by his Attorney and it appearing that the Defendant having had Legal Notice and the Court having considered the sd Motion, It is the Opinion of the Court that the Plaintiff recover of the sd Defendants the sum of one hundred & sixty four pounds nine Shillings and one penny Current money also his Costs by him in this behalf expended & the Defendt. be in Mercy etc.

RICHARD BUCKNER, JOHN BUCKNER, FRANCIS TALIAFERRO and GEORGE CATLETT or any three of them being first sworn do appraise all and Singular the Estate of ROBERT CALL deceased and make their Report to the next Court

In Obedience to an Order of Court held for Caroline County the 9th day of February 1764 We the Subscribers have viewed the way petitoned for by JAMES REYNOLDS for a Road from ELIAS BLACKURNs to DICKEYs Quarter and we find it may be made as good a way for the Publick and believe it to be a nearer way then where the Road now goes & it appears to us not to be of prejudiced to any Person adjoyning, THOS. CRUTCHER, WM. HORD, ELIAS BLACKBURN, THOMAS SALE. The Court having considered the Report

Ordered that the sd Road be established according to the above Report

AMBROSE HORD produced a Commission from his Honour the Governour to be Captain who having taken the Oaths to his Majesty's Person & Government subscribed the same with the Test

Page 59. Caroline County Court 8 March 1764

WILLIAM HORD presented a Commission from his Honour the Governour appointing him Lieutenant of a Company whereof AMBROSE HORD is Captain who having taken the Oaths to his Majesty's Person & Government Subscribed the same with the Test

HENRY STEWART presented a Commission from his Honour the Governour to be Ensign of a Company whereof AMBROSE HORD is Captain who having taken the Oaths to his Majesty's Person & Government subscribed the same with the Test

On the Petion of AQUILLA JOHNSTON his Ordinary License is renewed who with JOSEPH HIPPO his Security acknowledged their Bond for the same.

An Indenture of Apprenticeship from JOHN McCLAIRANE to JOSEPH STREET being first approved of by the Court was ordered to be recorded

An Indenture of Apprenticeship from DANIEL McCLAIRANE to JOSEPH STREET being first approved of by the Court was ordered to be recorded

LUNSFORD LOMAX JUNR. Gent took the usual Oaths to his Majesty's Person & Government as also the Oaths of a Justice of Peace at Common Law & Chancery subscribed the same with the Test

Present LUNSFORD LOMAX Gent

Page 60. Caroline County Court 8 March 1764.

We find the Road Petitioned for by GEORGE MEASE very little Inferiour to the old way when cleared. March 2d 1764. THOMAS SLAUGHTER, THOMAS SAMUEL, JOHN LONG. The Court having considered the above Report ordered that the sd Road be Established

JOHN TAYLOR Plaintiff against THOMAS COLAND Deft. In Debt

And now at this Day came the Deft. the sd THOMAS COLAND in his proper Person and says he cannot deny but all and every thing in the sd Planti. Declaration aforesd alledged are true nor but he owes the sd Plt. the sum of Eighteen pounds two shillings Current money like as the sd Plt. in his Declaration aforesd against him complains, Therefore it is considered by the Court that the Plantiff recover against the sd Deft the aforesd sum of Eighteen pounds two shillings Current money and also his Costs by him in this behalf expended & the sd Deft. be in Mercy etc.

This Judgment except the Costs to be discharged on the Defendants paying nine pounds one shilling Current money (remainder of this entry faded out)

JOHN YOUNGER Mercht. Plt. against WILLIAM JOHNSTON etc. Defts. On Motion This day came the Parties aforesd by their Attorneys and the Court having heard the matter on both sides

Page 61. Caroline County Court 8 March 1764

It is considered by the Court that the Plaintiff recover of the sd Defendant WILLIAM JOHNSTON the sum of two hundred and ninety one pounds ( )shillings and three pence half penny current money and also his Costs by him in this behalf expended & the Deft. be in Mercy etc. FRANCIS COLEMAN one of the Defts. in this Suit is discontinued

NB This Judgmt except the Costs is to be discharged on the payment of one hundred & ninety two pounds six Shillings with Interest at the rate of 5 per ct per ann: from the

20th day of July 1763 till paid

On the Petition of JOHN JOHNSTON to keep an Ordinary Licence is granted him on giving Bond & Security in the Office who with ROBERT WOOLFOLK his Security acknowledged their Bond for the same

Ordered that RICHARD SNEED, HUGH CROUCHER & their ganges be added to the Ganges formerly appointed to clear the Road to the new GLEEBE from thence to Colo. JOHN BAYLORs MILL along the old Road unless a better way can be found

A Deed from MAXIMILIAN BERRYMAN and MARY his Wife Indented to EDWARD DIXON the sd MARY being privately Examined by Vertue of a Commission thereto annexed was proved by the Oaths of three of the Witnesses & admitted to record

A Deed Indented from THOMAS LENDRUM & NELLY his Wife to THOMAS SCOTT was acknowledged by the sd THOMAS and proved by the Oath of ARCHIBALD CLARK as to the said NELLY

On the Motion of PLEASANT TERREL It is Ordered that JOHN THOMPSON, JAMES GATEWOOD & ROBERT MICKLEBERRY being first sworn before a Justice of the Peace for this County view the Road Petioned for by the sd TERREL & make Report therof to the next Court

An Indenture of Apprenticeship from BENJA. PANNEL to JOHN MARSHALL being first approved of by the Court was admitted to record

Page 62. Caroline County Court 8 March 1764

David a Negro Man Slave belonging to ROBERT TALIAFERRO Gent being brought before the Court & being charged with feloniously stealing and killing a Hog the property of JAMES REYNOLDS pleaded not Guilty upon Examining the Witnesses The opinion of the Court that the Sheriff take the sd David to the Publick Whipping Post and give him thirty nine lashes on his bare Back well laid on & be thence discharged

A Mortgage from JAMES GOUGE to JOHN YOUNGER was proved by the Oath of JOHN HINDE & ordered to be recorded

JOHN YOUNGER against WILLIAM JOHNSTON this WILLIAM having given JAMES JOHNSTON Security for stay of selling his goods by Virute of an Execution for three Months agreeable to an Act of Assembly in such cases made and provided objected to the sd JOHN YOUNGER having a Judgment against him because the sd JAMES one of the Obligon had not Legal Notice of the Motion which the Court overruled

Messrs. BOSWORTH & GRIFFITH Plts. against LUNSFORD LOMAX Gent Deft. In Debt Now at this day came LUNSFORD LOMAX JUR. Gent and undertook for LUNSFORD LOMAX Senr. Gent that in case he should be cast in this Suit he would satisfie and pay the condemnation of the Court or render his Body to Prison for Execution for the same or that he the sd LUNSFORD LOMAX JUR. would do it for him

WILLIAM NORMENT Plt. against JOHN NORMENT & JAMES DEJARNETT Deft In Debt The Sheriff having returned that the sd Defts. were not found Now at this day came the sd JOHN NORMENT in his proper person & says that he cannot deny but that all & every things in the sd Plaintiffs Declaration aforesaid are true nor but that he owes the sd Plaintiff the sum of Twenty

Page 63. Caroline County Court 8 March 1764

pounds Nine Shillings current money like as the said Plaintiff in his Declaration aforesd against him complains Therefore it is considered by the Court that the sd Plaintiff recover against the sd Defendt. the aforesd sum of Twenty pounds Nine Shillings current money and also his costs by him in this behalf expended & the Defendt. be in

Mercy etc

Memorandum This Judgment except the Costs is to be discharged on the payment of Ten pounds & four Shillings and six pence current money with Interest thereon from the Tenth day of October 1763 till paid

Then the Court adjourned till to Morrow morning 9 O' Clock
ROBERT GILCHRIST

At a Court continued and held for Caroline County on Friday March the 9th 1764
Present EDMUND PENDLETON, ROBERT GILCHRIST, JAMES JAMESON, JAMES TAYLOR, JOHN TAYLOR and JOHN BAYNHAM Gent Justices

JOHN SEMPLE etc against JOHN WALLER Now at this day came JOHN ROY & GEORGE STUBBLEFIELD into Court and undertook for the sd JOHN WALLER that in case he should be cast in this suit they the sd JOHN & GEORGE would do it for him & the aforesd Defendt. by ZACHERY LEWIS his Attorney comes and Defends the force and Injury whence And saith that he this Deft. did not assume in manner & form the sd Plt. in his Declaration aforesd against him Complains & says that this may be inquired of

Page 64. Caroline County Court 9 March 1764

by the Country and the sd Plaintiff likewise therefore let a Jury thereof come at the next Court etc.

BENJAMIN WINSLOW Plt. against JOHN WALLER Deft. Now at this Day came JOHN BEVERLEY ROY & GEORGE STUBBLEFIELD into Court and undertook for the sd JOHN that in case he should be cast in this Suit they would satisfie & pay the condemnation of the Court or render his Body to Prison in Execution for the same or that they the sd JOHN & GEORGE would do it for him & the aforesaid Defendant by ZACHERY LEWIS his Attorney comes and Defends the force and Injury whence and saith that the Plaintiff his action aforesd thereof against him ought not to have & maintain because he saith He hath well and truly paid the sd Plt. the aforesd (blank) pounds & according to the form Effect of the Bond aforesd & prays that this may be enquired of by the Country & the sd Plt likewise therefore let a Jury thereof come at the next Court etc.

FRANCIS SMITH Plt. against FRANCS. FLEMING. JOHN ELLIOT PAINE came into Court & undertook for the sd FRANCIS that in case he should be cast in the suit that he would satisfie and pay the condemnation of the Court or render his Body to Prison in Execution for the same or that he the sd JOHN would do it for him

PHILIP MAY Plt. Against WILLIAM WALLER Deft. JOHN WALLER came into Court and undertook for the sd WILLIAM that in case he should be cast in this Suit that he would satisfie & pay the condemnation of the Court or render his Body to Prison in Execution for the same or that he the sd JOHN would do it for him

LAWRENCE TALIAFERRO against FRANCIS TALIAFERRO In Chancery
This Suit is continued

Page 65. Caroline County Court 9 March 1764

JOHN GRIFFIN Complt. against NICHOLAS LONG Deft General Replication Commission

WILLIAM SMITH against SARAH SMITH etc. In Chancery

The Court hearing the Bill Answer etc Ordered and Decreed that the sd Complainant be put in possession of the Land that the Defendant SARAH convey her Dower & that the Infant BRUTON SMITH shall in six Months after he arrives to the age of twenty one years convey the sd thirty five or forty acres mentioned in the sd Complts. Bill to the sd Complt. in Fee Simple or shew cause to the Contrary & that the Defts. pay the Plaint. his costs by him in this behalf expended

FRANCIS COLEMAN against JAMES FARISH Deft. In Debt

This Suit is agreed Dismissed

REUBIN BROWN Plt. against EDWARD POWER Deft. is contd.

WILLIAM COPLAND & COMPY. Plts. against WILLIAM BOWLER Deft.

On the motion ROBERT ARMISTEAD OLIVER TOWLES JR. entered himself in this Suit security for the costs

THOMAS BRIDGFORTH Plt. against FRANCIS THORPE Deft.

This Suit continued for Report

WILLIAM SPILLER Plt. against CHARLES CARTER JUNR. Deft

This Suit is Contd

Present WILLIAM PARKER Gent

JAMES MILLER Plt. against JAMES TALIAFERRO Deft.

This Suit being referr'd is continued for Report

COLLIN (blurred)DOCK Plt. agst JAMES TALIAFERRO Deft.

This Suit being refered is continued for Report

JOHN MILLER Plt. agst. EDWARD POWERS Deft. This Suit is continued

Page 66. Caroline County Court 9 March 1764

FRANCIS THORPE Plaintiff against REUBIN BROWN Defendts. In Debt

The Defendants having waived their Pleas Judgment is granted the Plaintiff against the sd Defendants BROWN & JOHN WYNALD SAUNDERS the sum of thirty pounds three Shillings and six pence current money and also his Costs by him in this behalf expended the said Defendant be in Mercy etc.

Memorandum This Judgment except the costs is to be discharged on the Payment of fifteen pounds & one Shilling & nine pence current money with lawfull Interest thereon from the 10th day of September 1761 till paid

JAMES FARISH Plt. against THOMAS JONES Trespass Assault & Battery

Suit is dismissed with costs

JOHN BARNES against PETER LANTOR in Detinue This Suit is dismissed

EDWARD POWERS Plt. against LUNSFORD LOMAX Deft. In Case

Now at this day came the parties aforesaid by their Attorneys and thereupon a Jury to Wit ABRAHAM HARPER & were impannelled & sworn well and truly to try the matter in issue joined who having heard the Arguments and Evidences of each Party and in a short time returned the following Verdict. We the Jury find for the Plt. Thirteen pounds sixteen Shillings and five pence Current money. ABRAHAM HARPER Foreman. which Verdict on the Plts. Motion is recorded And it is considered by the Court that the Plt recover the aforesaid sum of money and also his Costs by him in this behalf expended

MAURICE SMITH Plt against JAMES LITTLEPAGE Deft.

This Suit is Continued for Report

PAUL THILMAN against GEORGE PEAY. This Suit is contd.

Page 67. Caroline County Court 9 March 1764

THOMAS REYNOLDS against REYNOLDS McKINNY. This Suit is continued

ROY's Exors. against ALLANs Exors. This Suit is referred to ROBERT GILCHRIST Gent his Award to be the Judgment of the Court

JAMES BOWIE against WILLIAM KING. This Suit is continued

LUCRETIA SALMAN against ROBERT FARISH. This Suit is continued at the Plaintiffs Costs

NICHOLAS MULLIN against ROBERT FARISH. This Suit is cont'd and it is Ordered a Dedimus be Issued to take the Deposition of JANE WATTS De bene esse on giving the Deft. legal notice of the same

CHARLES CULLIN Plaint. against JAMES FARISH Defendt. In Debt

And Now at this Day came the partys aforesaid by their Attorneys and thereupon also came a Jury to Wit THOMAS CROUCHER & were impannelled and sworn well and truly to try the matter in Issue Joyned who having heard the arguments & Evidences of each Party withdrew and in a short time returned the following Verdict. We of the Jury do find for the Plt. five pounds current money THOMAS CROUCHER Foreman, which Verdict on the Plaint. motion is recorded And it is considered by the Court that the Plt. recover of the sd Deft. the aforesd sum of money and also his costs in this behalf expended & the sd Deft. be in Mercy etc.

WILLIAM JOHNSTON Assee. Plt. against BENJAMIN CATLETT Deft. In Debt

Now at this Day came the Partys aforesaid by their Attorneys who have argued the Plea and Demurrer It is considered by the Court that the sd Plt recover of the sd Defendant the sum of Eight pounds current money with lawfull Interest from the 6th day of March 1761 till paid and also his Costs by him in this behalf expended the sd Deft in Mercy etc.

PHILIP MAY Plt. against JAMES JOHNSTON Deft. In Case

And now this day came the Partys aforesd by their Attorneys and thereupon came a Jury to wit GEORGE TODD & were impannelled and sworn well and truly to try the matter in Issue Joined who having heard the arguments

Page 68. Caroline County Court 9 March 1764

and Evidence of each party withdrew and in a short time returned this following Verdict. We the Jury do find for the Plaintiff Ten pounds ten shillings current money GEORGE TODD Foreman. which verdict at the plaintiffs motion is recorded and it is considered by the Court that the Plaintiff recover of the said Defendant the aforesaid sum of money and also his costs by him in this behalf expended and the said Defendant be in Mercy etc.

WILLIAM CHICK Plaintiff against WILLIAM BOWLER Deft. In Case

And now at this day came the parties aforesd by their Attorneys and thereupon a Jury to wit GEORGE TODD & were impannelled and sworn well and truly to trie the matter in Issue Joined who haveing heard the arguments and Evidence of each partie withdrew and in a short time returned the following verdict. We the Jury do find for the Plaintiff Fourteen pounds six Shillings and ten pence half penny current money which Verdict on the Plaintiffs motion is recorded and it is considered by the Court that the Plaintiff recover of the said Defendant the aforesaid sum of money and also his costs by him in this behalf expended and the Defendant be in mercy etc

Its ordered PHILL MAY pay GEORGE WILY Seventy five pounds of Tobo. for three days attendance as an Evidence for him against JOHNSTON

It ordered WILLIAM CHICK pay LAWRENCE SMITH fifty pounds of Tobacco for 2 days attendance as an Evidence for him against BOWLER

Its Ordered JAMES TAYLOR Gent pay DOCTOR JOHN WALKER Fifteen Shillings that he expended in apprehending Tom a Negroe man Slave belonging to HENRY GILBERT of HANOVER COUNTY as soon as he receives the County cash

Page 69. Caroline County Court 9 March 1764

JAMES GEORGE Plt against RICHARD ROE Deft. In Debt
Now at this Day came the parties aforesd by their Attorneys and the said Defendant having waved his plea Judgment is granted the Plaintiff against the said Defendant the sum of Twenty two pounds Ten Shillings Currt. money Therefore it is ordered by the Court that the Plaintiff recover of the said Defendt. the aforesaid sum of money as also his costs by him in this behalf expended and the sd be in mercy etc.

JAMES RITCHIE Plt. agst. JOHN BOWCOCK Deft. In Debt
This day came the parties by their Attorneys who mutally agreed to wave the Issue on the Country and Submit the matter to the Judgment of the Court whereupon all and singular the premises being seen and by the Court fully understood its considered that the Plaintiff recover against the said Defendant the sum of one hundred and two pounds and also his costs by him in this behalf expended and the said Deft be in mercy etc This Judgment except the costs is to be discharged on the payment of fifty one pounds Eight shillings and five pence Currt. money with Interest from the twelfth day of March 1761 till paid

Its Ordered PHILIP MAY pay JAMES REYNOLDS one hundred and twenty five pounds of Tobacco for 5 days attendance as an Evidence for him against JOHNSTON

Page 70. Caroline County Court 9 March 1764

JOHN MILLER Plaintiff against GILLISONs Executors Deft.
(entry partly missing) . . This Suit is referred . . . . . GRAY, EDWARD DIXON & JAMES BOWIE or any two of them and their Award shall be the Judgment of this Court

JOSIAH ( ) an Evidence of CHARLES CULLENS against JAMES FARISH he having attended four days Its ordered the said CULLIN pay him one hundred pounds of Tobacco for the same

NATHANIEL RITCHISON Plt. against PETER LANTOR Deft. In Debt
This Suit is continued

MOZA HURT Plt. agt. SAMUELL NORMENT Deft. In Trespass
And now this day came the parties by their Attorney and thereupon came also a Jury to wit JOHN JONES etc who being elected tryed and sworn the truth to speak upon the issue joined and having heard the arguments and evidences of each partie withdrew and in a short time returned the following Verdict. We of the Jury do find for the Deft. JOHN JONES Foreman which Verdict at the Defendants motion is recorded Whereupon it is considered by the Court that the Plaintiff take nothing by his Bill but for his false clamour be in mercy and that the said Deft. go thereof without day and recover against the said Plaintiff his costs by him about his defence in this behalf expended

ARCHIBALD McCALL agt. JOHN WILY Debt. This Suit is continued

Page 71. Caroline County Court 9 March 1764

Its Ordered CHARLES CULLEN pay JOHN JOHNSTON fifty pounds of Tobacco for two days attendance as an Evidence for him against JAMES FARISH

JOHN GRAY Plt. agst. FRANCIS STERN Deft. In Debt. Demurr &

Its Ordered that SAMUELL NORMENT pay THOMAS JAMES one hundred and fifty pounds of Tobacco for six days attendance as an Evidence for him at the suit of HURT

Its ordered that SAMUELL NORMENT pay MILLY JONES one hundred and twenty five pounds of Tobacco for five days attendance as an evidence for him at the Suit of HURT

Its ordered that MOZA HURT pay JOHN NORMENT one hundred and fifty pounds of Tobacco for six days attendance as an Evidence for him agst SAMUELL NORMENT

Its ordered that SAMUEL NORMENT pay FRANCIS LANKFORD one hundred and twenty five pounds of Tobacco for five days attendance as an evidence for him at the Suit of HURT

Its ordered that MOZA HURT pay THOMAS ARTHUR fifty pounds of Tobo. for two days attendance as an Evidence for him against NORMENT

JOHN GRAY etc. Plts. against JOHN WILY Defendant In Debt

This day came the parties by there Attorneys who mutually agreed to wave the Issue to the Contrey and submitted the matter to the Judgment of the Court whereupon all and singular the premises being seen and by the Court fully understood its considered by the Court that the Plaintiff recover against the said Defendant

Page 72. Caroline County Court 9 March 1764

thirty eight pounds Sixteen shillings and three pence the debt in the Declaration mentioned and also his costs by him in this behalf expended. This Judgment (the costs excepted) is to be discharged by the payment nineteen pounds eight shillings and one penny half penny current money with lawfull interest thereon after the rate of 5 p ct p annum from the twenty fifth day of August 1761 till paid

JOHN YOUNGER Plt. against JOHN YOUNG Defendt. Trespass on the Case

Now this day came the parties aforesaid by their Attorneys and thereupon came a Jury to wit WILLIAM HOWARD etc & being impannelled and sworn well and truly to try the matter in issue Joined who haveing heard the argument and evidences of each partie withdrew and in a short time returned the following Verdict. We of the Jury do find for the Plaintiff Twelve pounds current money WILLIAM HOWARD foreman which Verdict at the Plaintiffs motion is recorded, therefore it is considered by the Court the Plaintiff recover of the said Deft. the aforesaid sum of money and also his costs by him in this behalf expended and the said Deft. may be taken etc

WILLIAM, JOHN and ELIZABETH HALBERT with the Approbation of the Court made choice of FRANCIS HALBERT as their Guardian who acknowledged a bond for the same

In the Suit on the Attachment obtained by JOHN ELLIOT PAINE Plt. against (blank) BATES Deft WILLIAM CHICK being sworn as Garnishee in this Suit declared he had in his hands one and a half bushells of Corn and an old Bed Stead and the Defendant is indebted to him eight shillings, it is ordered that he deliver the said Effects to the Sherif in order that they may be sold

Ordered that the Court be adjourned till tomorrow morng. 9 O'clock

EDMUND PENDLETON

Page 73. Caroline County Court 10 March 1764

At a Court held for Caroline County on Saturday the 10th of March 1761 for the Examination of ROBERT BERNATT on suspicion of Forgery

Present EDMUND PENDLETON ROBERT GILCHRIST
JOHN TAYLOR, WILLIAM PARKER & JOHN BAYNHAM Gent Justices

ROBERT BERNATT being committed to the Goal of the County by a Mittimus from under the hand of ROBERT GILCHRIST Gent one of his Majesties Justices of the peace for the sd County on Suspicion of felony in Counterfeit or forging and sending payment some Treasury notes being brought before the Court for examination pleaded not guilty on hearing and examining the witnesses against him its the opinion of the Court that the facts against him are so sufficiently proved as that he may thereupon have a further tryall before the next General Court and its therefore ordered that the said ROBERT

BERNATT be remanded back to the Goal of this County and the Sherif of the sd County as soon as conveniantly remove the said BERNATT to the publick Goal of this Colony in the City of WILLIAMSBURGH in order to have his further tryall before the Judges of the Generall Court

GABRIEL TOOMBS, EDWARD POWERS, JOHN BROADDUS & JOHN EMMERSON severally acknowledged themselves Indebted to our Sovereign Lord the King in the sum of Fifty pounds each to be Levied on their respective lands and goods and to the use of our Lord the King rendered in case each of them do not appear before the Judges of the Generall Court at the Capitoll in WILLIAMSBURG on the sixth day of the next Court to give evidence agt ROBERT BERNATT for felony or depart thence without leave of the sd Court EDMD. PENDLETON

Page 74. Caroline County Court 10 March 1764

At a Court held for Caroline County on Saturday the 10th day of March 1764
Present EDMUND PENDLETON, ROBERT GILCHRIST,
JOHN TAYLOR, WILLIAM PARKER & JNO. BAYNHAM Gent Justices

The Inventory and appraisement of the Estate of ROBT. KAY deceased was this day returned and admitted to record

Its Ordered that JAMES TERRELL, JACOB BURRAS, DAVID STERN and JOHN HAMPTON or any three of them being first duly sworn according to Law do settle and lay of one fourth part of the Estate of WILLIAM STONE deceased for his Widow MARY STONE

On the Petition of WILLIAM POE and THOMAS RENNOLDS for ELIZABETH CHARLES giving Counter Security and she failing to Comply with the sd Order its ordered she deliver up the whole estate of OLIVER CHARLES deceased to WILLIAM POE and THOS. RENNOLDS

The Court proceeded to rate the liquors and make the following alteration

Rum	10 p gallon
Hott Meal	1.s
Strong Bear	1.6

Stableage and eight bundles of good fodder 0.7 1/2 and so in proportion

JAMES TERRELL against JOHN ALMAND. This Suit is continued for Report

HARRY BEVERLEY Plt. against ROBERT KAY Deft. In Chancery
This Suit abates at the Defts. Death

JNO. WINL. SANDERS against WILLIAM JORDAN. In Chancery
General Replication & Comm.

Page 75. Caroline County Court 10 March 1764

RICHARD BERNARD Plt. against OLIVER TOWLES Respondt. In Chancery
This Suit is dismissed

ZACHARY COGHILL against THOMAS DICKINSON Replication & Comm.

DANIEL BARKSDALE against ABRAHAM WILLSON In Chancery
Continued for Rept.

JOHN GRAY et al against ROBERT ROBERTS et al In Chancery
This Suit is continued

JAMES GATEWOOD against WILLIAM HEWLETT. In Chancery
This Suit is continued for report

RICHARD WOOLFOLK against WILLIAM JOHNSTON. In Chy.
The Defendant having failed to give in his answer its ordered that an attachment issue unless he does it in a week

ROBERT GARRETT Plaintff. against BENJAMIN CATLETT Respondt. In Chancery Dismissed Agreed

JOHN FORD Plt. against ANN GOUCH Respondt. In Chancery This Suit is dismissed being agreed

ROBERT GILCHRIST Plt. against BENJAMIN CATLETT Respondt. In Chancery This suit is dismissed being agreed

HARRY BEVERLEY Compl̃t. against JOHN FIELDING Defendt. In Chancery This Suit being referr'd to EDWARD DIXON, ROBERT GILCHRIST & JOHN GRAY returned their report as follows.

1755 HARRY BEVERLEY to JOHN FIELDING	Do
To Sundry Quantities of Beef at several times	2..15..7
To 5 gallons of Brandy	1..-----

Page 76. Caroline County Court 10 March 1764

To rope for the Schooner'		0..5..0
To a sack		0..4..0
To a horse 60/ ten giese @ 1/3		3..12..6
To 2 Broad Hoes 3/ a plow hoe 3/		0..6..0
To 4 Turkeys		0..5..0
To 8 1/2 barrells Corn 11/		4..5..0
To 1 hilling hoe 3/6; 1 narrow axe 4/8		0..8..2
To MARY FIELDS for washing, makeing, mending etc some of which we have not allowed		10..0..0
By sundrys per account delivered by HARRY BEVERLEY and agreed to by FIELDING		(blurred)
By a hogg 54 lb @ 2d		(blurred)
By ballance due JOHN FIELDING		1..4..6
	23...1...3	
To Balla. p Contra due JNO. FIELDING	1...4...6	
To Corn & Tobacco omitted	8...3...1	9...7...7

In Obedience to an Order of the Worshipfull Court of Caroline dated the 10 of September we the Subscribers having heard the parties and examined the accounts have settled the same as above and do find that HARRY BEVERLEY Justly Indebted to JOHN FIELDING th sum of Nine pounds Seven shillings and seven pence which we award the sd BEVERLEY to pay and are of opinion that the said BEVERLEY should pay the costs of the Suit but that we Submitt to the Worshipfull Court Witness our hands this 10 September 1763. The Court on considering the report its ordered and decreed that on the Plaintiffs paying the said Defendant the sum of Nine pounds Seven shillings and seven pence Currt. money and also his costs as well at Common Law as in equity the sd Injunction be perpetual

Page 77. Caroline County Court 10 March 1764

JACOB WOODLEY Complt. against OLIVER TOWLES Respondt. In Chancery This Suit dismissed being agreed

(blank) Complt. against (blank) BUCKNER Respondt. In Chancery This Suit is dismissed being agreed

(blank) CHANDLER Complt. against (blank) SOUTHWORTH Respondt. This Suit is continued (blank) STEVENS Complt. against HUNTERs Exors. Respondt. This Suit is continued for answer

JOHN GRAY Plt. against. MARY CATLETT Deft. Trespass on the Case. Now at this day came the parties aforesaid by their Attorneys and thereupon a Jury to witt JOHN BOWCOCK & being impannelled and sworn well and truly to try the matter in Issue joined who having heard the arguments and evidence of each partie withdrew and in a short time returned the following Verdict. We the Jury do find for the Plaintiff (blurred) pounds thirteen shillings and one half penny Curt. money JOHN BOWCOCK Foreman. which Verdict at the Plaintiffs motion is recorded Whereupon it is considered by the Court that the Plt recover against the said Deft. the aforesaid sum of money as also his costs by him in this behalf expended and the Deft be in Mercy etc.

JOHN GRAY etc. Plt. against JOHN BILLOPS Deft. Trespass on the Case This day came the parties afaoresaid by their Attorneys who mutually agreed to wave the issue to the Countrey and submitted the matter to the Judgmt. of the Court Whereupon all and singular the premises being seen and by the Court fully understood that the Plaintiff

Page 78. Caroline County Court 10th March 1764

recover against the said Defendant the sum of Six pounds Eight Shillings Currt. money and his costs by him in this behalf expended and the Defendant being in Mercy etc.

JOHN GRAY etc. Plt. against JAMES BOWLER JUNR. Deft. Trespass on the Case Now at this day came the parties aforesaid by their Attorneys and thereupon a Jury to Wit JOHN BROADDUS etc. be impannelled and sworn well and truly to try the matter in Issue Joined who having heard the arguments and evidence of each party withdrew and in a short time returned the following Verdict. We of the Jury find for the Plaintiff five pounds six Shillings and five pence Damages JOHN BROADDUS Foreman which Verdict at the plaintiffs motion is recorded and whereupon its considered by the Court that the Plt recover against the said Defendant the aforesaid sum of money as also his costs by him in this behalf expended and the Defendant be in mercy etc.

On the petition of JOHN MILLER its ordered his Ordinary Licence be renewed he having given bond & sufficient Security for the same

Ordered that the Court be adjourned till the Court in Course

At a Court held for Caroline County on Thursday the 12th day of Apl. 1764
Present ROBERT GILCHRIST, JAMES JAMESON
ROBERT TALIAFERRO, & JOHN TAYLOR Gentlemen Justices

An Account of the Estate of JOHN CLARKE deceased was this day returned and admitted to record

BENJAMIN LONG acknowledged his Deed of Lease to HENRY WARE and its admitted to record

Page 79. Caroline County Court 12th April 1764

The Last Will and Testament of DANIEL TOMPKINS deceased was presented in Court by CHRISTOPHER TOMPKINS and JAMES TOMPKINS Executors therein named who made Oath thereto according to Law, and being further proved by the oaths of the Witnesses is admitted to record, and the said Exors. having performed what was usual in such cases, Certificate is granted them for obtaining a probate in due form of Law, a Bond acknowledged etc.

Its Ordered that GABRIEL THROCKMORTON, WILLIAM TYLER, JOHN CLARK & ROGER QUARLES or any three of them being first sworn according to Law appraise the Estate of DANIEL TOMPKINS deceased and make report of their proceedings to the next Court and also devide the Estate according to the Will & according to Law

JOSIAH TOMPKINS Orphan of DANIEL TOMPKINS deceased being this day admitted to chuse a Guardian made choice of JAMES TOMPKINS who acknowledged a bond for the same

ANN and SUSANAH TOMPKINS being this day admitted to chuse a Guardian makes choice of JAMES TOMPKINS who was approved of by the Court bond acknowledged etc.

WILLIAM MOTTLEY and ELIZABETH his Wife she being first privately examined ackowledged their Deed indented to THOMAS BROADDUS and its admitted to record

Its ordered that WILLIAM QUARLES be overseer of the Road from the Road that leads to their Mines to QUARLES MILL and FOARD, & PLEASANT JERRELLs, WILLIAM GOODALLs and WILLIAM QUARLES hands do work on the same and keep it in repair according to Law

The Last Will and Testament and Codicil of NICHOLAS BATTAILE Gent deceased was presented in Court by WILLIAM WOODFORD Gent one of the Exors. therein named who made oath thereto according to law and being further proved by the Oaths of three of the witnesses thereto and admitted to record, and the said Executor performing what is usual in such cases, Certificate is granted him for obtaining a probate in due form of Law and acknowledged a bond for the same

Page 80. Caroline County Court 12th April 1764

Its Ordered that RICHARD BUCKNER, WILLIAM ALCOCK, BENJAMIN ROBINSON JUNR. and SETH THORNTON or any three of them being first sworn before a Justice of the peace for this County do appraise the Estate of NICHOLAS BATTAILE Gent. deceased and make report of their proceedings to the next Court

Its Ordered that JOHN SLAUGHTER, JOHN SLAUGHTER, JAMES BENNERLEY and R-- (?) BURGIN or any two of them being first sworn according to Law appraise the Estate of NICHOLAS BATTAILE deceased in CULPEPER and return their proceedings to the next Court.

Its Ordered that the Churchwardens of St. Margaretts Parish bind out ANN and SUSANNAH TOMPKINS Orphans of DANIEL TOMPKINS deceased according to law.

The Last Will and Testament of JOHN MARTIN deceased was presented in Court by ISABELL MARTIN Executrix therein named who made oath thereto according to law and was further proved by the oaths of FRANCIS (blurred) & ABRAHAM MARTIN witnesses and its admitted to record, & the said Executrix performing what is usual in such cases Certificate is granted her for obtaining a probate in due form of Law, bond acknowledged etc.

Its Ordered that CHRISTOPHER SINGLETON, EDWARD ROWSIE, CHARLES BEASLEY and JOHN SNEED or any three of them being first sworn before a Justice of the peace for this County do appraise the Estate of JOHN MARTIN deceased and make report of their proceedings to Court

CHARLES BURRUS and SALLY his Wife etc. she being first privately examined acknowledged their said Indenture to WILLIAM TYLER and ordered to be recorded

ELIJAH DANIEL and MARY his Wife acknowledged their Deed of Gift to their Daughter AGNIS ARNOLD which is admitted to record

The Last Will and Testament of JOHN HOLLOWAY deceased was presented in Court by ELIZA. and JOHN HOLLOWAY Executrx. & Exor. therein named who made oath according to law and was further proved by the oaths of three of the witnesses & admd. to record, & the Exx. & Exr. performg. what is usual in such cases Certificate is granted them for obtaining a probate thereof in due form of law, bonds acknd., etc.

Page 81. Caroline County Court 12th April 1764

On the motion of GILES SAMUEL, JAMES PATTIE and WILLIAM POE, Ordered that JAMES GOUGE give Counter Security as Guardian of JNO. GOUGE

JOHN BUCKNER SENR. acknowledged his deed Indented to JOHN BUCKNER Younger and its admitted to record

MATTHEW PETROSS acknowledged his Deed Indented to JAMES BOWIE was proved by oaths of ARCHIBALD CLARK, PATRICK COCKRAM and EDWARD DIXON witnesses thereto and admitted to record

Its Ordered that JONATHAN DOUGLAS be clear of his Indenture which he entered into with JOHN SALMON and that the Churchwardens of St. Margarets Parish bind out the said SALMON according to Law

JOSEPH LANKFORD is appointed Guardian to JOSEPH, NICHOLAS and RICHARD BRIDGES Orphans of MORGAN BRIDGES deceased and acknowledged a bond for the same

Its Ordered that ANTHONY THORNTON, WILLIAM PARKER and JAMES TAYLOR Gent let the building of two prisons one for Criminals and the other for Debtors

ROSANAH GRANT Orphan of DANIEL GRANT deceased being this day admitted to chuse a Guardian makes choice of WILLIAM SAMUEL who is approved by the Court, Bond acknowledged etc.

The Last Will and Testament of MARY GOUGE deceased was presented in Court by JAMES GOUGE Administrator with the Will annexed and was proved by the oaths of the witnesses and admitted to record and the sd Administrator performing what is usual in such cases Certificate is granted him for obtaining a probate thereof in due form of law

Its Ordered that JOHN BOUTWELL, ROBERT GARRETT, RICHARD ALCOCK & SIMON MILLER or any three of them being first duly sworn acordg. to law appraise the Estate of MARY GOUGE deced and make report of their proceedings to next Court

Page 82. Caroline County Court 12th April 1764

JOHN BAIRD etc. Plts. against FRANCIS COLEMAN Deft. Case

This suit by consent of parties and the order of Caroline County Court being referred to the determination of JOHN BAYLOR & EDMUND PENDLETON Gent. & their award being returned in these words, We do award that the Plt. recover against the Deft twenty two pounds nineteen shillings and two pence & costs of JOHN BAYLOR & EDMUND PENDLETON which award the Court confirms and its ordered that the said FRAS. COLEMAN pay unto the sd Plt. the aforesaid sum of money and their costs by them in this behalf expended

JOHN BROWN Plt. against WILLIAM JOHNSTON Deft. Case

JOHN WALLER Special Bail and Imparlence

WILLIAM DICKINSON and ANN his Wife she being first privately examined acknowledged their Deed Indented to WILLIAM HEWLET, was further proved by the oath of BENJAMIN TOMPKINS a witness thereto and admitted to record

PETER HOWE Esqr. Assee. of JOHN CHAMPE Exor. etc. of COLO. CHAMPE deced Plt. against WILLIAM PARRY Defendt. This suit is dismissed

JAMES GOUGE Plt against JOHN CUMMING Deft. Case

This Suit is dismissed being agreed

In the Suit on the attachment obtained by ROBERT GILCHRIST Gent Plt. ACHILLES WHITLOCK Defendant Mr. TURNER being sworn as garnishee declared he has in his hands one hogshead of Tobacco weight one thousand one hundred and twenty eight and that the Defendant is indebted to him in the sum of Six pounds Ten shillings and its ordered that he sell the sd Tobo and be accountable to the further order of this Court

Page 83. Caroline County Court 12th April 1764

ARCHIBALD GORAN Plt. against JEREMIAH JORDAN Deft. On Attachment
The Defendant being solemnly called and failing to appear Judgt. is granted the Plt. against said Defendant for the sum of nineteen pounds fifteen shillings current money & also his costs by him in this behalf expended. This Judgment except the Costs is to be discharged on the payment of nine pounds seventeen shills. and six pence with lawfull Interest thereon after the rate of five per cent per annum from the tenth day of May one thousand seven hundred and sixty three untill the same be paid & the Sheriff having returned on the sd Attachment that he attached one negroe and its ordered that the Sheriff sell the said Negroe according to law and the money arising to go to the satisfaction of the said Judgment.

RICHARD TUNSTALL Plt. against GARRETT HACKETT Deft. On Petition
The Defendant appeared and confest Judgment to the Plt for the sum of four pounds Six shills. and seven pence current money which he is ordered to pay unto the sd Plt with an Attorneys fee & costs etc.

ZACHARY TALIAFERRO Plt. against CHARLES CARTER Esqr. Case
By consent of parties and with the Order of Caroline County Court this suit is referred to THOS. FITZHUGH, JOHN FITZHUGH, EDWARD DIXON, DEKAR TOMPSON & ARTHUR MORISON or any three of them being first sworn according to law to be determined the fifth day of June next and there award to be the Judgment of the Court

Its Ordered CHARLES CARTER pay ROBERT GREEN one hundred and ninety pounds of Tobacco for one days attendance and for coming and returning fifty five miles as an Evidence for him agst TALIAFERRO

Page 84. Caroline County Court 12th April 1764

JOHN BAYNHAM Plt. against JEREMIAH JORDAN Deft. On Attachment
This Suit is dismissed being agreed

BARTHOLOMEW CHEWNING Plt. against BENJAMIN WILLIAMSON On Attachment
This Suit is dismissed with costs etc.

THOMAS ELLIOTT Plt. against JOHN WILY Deft. Trespass on the Case
The Defendant came into Court and confest Judgment unto the said Plaintiff for thirteen pounds Currt. money which is ordered to pay unto the Plt. with costs etc. staying Execution till June next

BRYAN FITZPATRICK Plt. against JOHN PICKETT Deft. Case
This Suit is dismissed being agreed

FRANCIS COLEMAN Plt. against THOMAS TILLER Deft. In Debt
The Defendant being solemnly called and failing to appear Judgment is granted the Plt against the said Defendt. for his costs by him in this behalf expended etc.

Its Ordered ZACHARY TALIAFERRO pay THOMAS BALLARD one hundred & ninety five pounds of Tobacco for one days attendance and coming & returning fifty five miles as an evidence for him against CHARLES CARTER

Its Ordered ZACHARY TALIAFERRO pay JOHN WHITING eighty five pounds of Tobacco for one days attendance and coming and returning twenty miles from STAFFORD & two ferriages at PORT ROYAL as an Evidence for him against CARTER

Page 85. Caroline County Court 12th April 1764

Ordered ZACHARY TALIAFERRO pay BENETT ROWE five hundred and five pounds of Tobacco for one days attendance and coming and returning Sixty miles out of FAUQUIER and two ferriages at FALMOUTH as an Evidence for him against CHARLES CARTER

Ordered ZACHARY TALIAFERRO pay DAVID MASON two hundred and twenty pounds of Tobacco for 1 days attendance and coming and returning sixty five miles from FAUQUIER and two ferriages at HUNTERS as an evidence for him against CHARLES CARTER

Its Ordered ZACHARY TALIAFERRO pay JOHN SMITHER two hundred and five pounds of Tobo. for 1 days attendance & for coming and returning sixty miles and two ferriages as an Evidence for him against CHARLES CARTER

Its Ordered ZACHARY TALIAFERRO pay JOHN BARNES two hundred and two pounds of Tobacco for one days attendance and once coming and returning 59 miles and two ferriages as an evidence for him against CHARLES CARTER

Its Ordered ZACHARY TALIAFERRO pay EDWARD BALLENGER one hundred and forty five pounds of Tobacco for 1 days attendance and coming and returning (?)0 miles as an evidence for him agst CHARLES CARTER

Its Ordered ZACHARY TALIAFERRO pay BENJAMIN B(faded) (could be BALLARD) one hundred and thirty one pounds of Tobacco for one days attendance and for once coming & returning 37 miles and two ferriages as an evidence for him against CHARLES CARTER

Its Ordered ZACHARY TALIAFERRO pay THOMAS COLEMAN two hundred and five pounds of Tobo. for 1 days attendance and coming and returning 60 miles and two ferraiges as an evidence for him against CHARLES CARTER

Page 86. Caroline County Court 12th April 1764

Its Ordered ZACHARY TALIAFERRO pay RICHARD LEWIS ninety one pounds of Tobacco for 1 days attendance and coming and returning 26 miles and two ferriages as an evidence for him agst CHARLES CARTER

JOHN TAYLOR Plt. against JOHN ELLIOT PAINE etc. Deft. In Debt
The Defendant came into Court and confest Judgment to the said Plaintiff in the sum of Seven pounds seventeen shillings and five pence half penny current money which he is ordered to pay unto the said Plt. with costs etc.

ROBERT MICKLEBURROUGH Plt. against GARRETT HACKITT Deft. Debt
The Defendant being called and failing to appear Judgment is granted the Plt against the said Defendant for the sum of ten pounds eight shillings & half penny current money with Interest thereon from the first day of February 1762 untill the same be paid which he is ordered to pay to the Plt. with costs

Its Ordered a Grand jury be Summoned to appear at the next Court

Its Ordered the Court be adjourned till tomorrow morning 9 o'clock

ROBERT GILCHRIST

At a Court held for Caroline County on Ffriday the 13 day of April 1764
Present ANTHONYTHORNTON, JAMES TAYLOR
WILLIAM PARKER & JOHN TAYLOR Gentlemen Justices

Page 87. Caroline County Court 13th April 1764

JOHN RICHARDS Plt. against ACHILES FOSTER Deft. In Debt

This day came the aforesaid Defendant and says that he cannot deny the writing obligatory in the declaration mentioned nor but he owes the said Plaintiff the sum of thirty three pounds Thirteen shillings and four pence like as the said Plaintiff against him complains Therefore its considered by the Court that the Plaintiff recover of the said Defendant the aforesaid sum of money and also his costs by him in this behalf expended

The judgment except the Costs is to be discharged on the payment of Sixteen pounds Sixteen shillings and eight pence current money with lawfull Interest thereon after the rate of 5 per cent per annum from the 16 day of December 1762 untill paid

WILLIAM LYNE against MARK MARRIOTT and JOHN MOTLEY Defts. In Debt

This day came the aforesaid Defendants and says they cannott deny the writing obligatory in the declaration mentioned nor but they owe the said Plaintiff the sum of twenty six pounds seven shillings and six pence like as the said Plantiff against them complains Therefore its considered by the Court that the Plaintiff recover against the Defendant the aforesaid sum of money as also his costs by him in this behalf expended

This Judgment except the costs to be discharged by the payment of Thirteen pounds three shillings & nine pence current money with Interest thereon from the 6th day of July 1763 till paid

Page 88. Caroline County Court 13th April 1764

An Account of the Administration of the Estate of ROBERT HALL deceased was this day returned and admitted to record

WILLIAM LYNE Plt. against JOHN MOTHLEY Deft for Debt

This day came the aforesaid Defendant and says he cannot deny the writing obligatory in the Declaration mentioned nor but he owes the said Plaintiff the sum of fourteen pounds two shillings like as the said Plaintif against him complains Therefore it is considered by the Court that the Plt. recover of the said Defendant the aforesaid sum of money as also his costs by him in this behalf expended

ThisJudgment except the costs is to be discharged on the payment of seven pounds one shilling with Lawfull Interest thereon after the rate of 5 per cent per annum from the sixth day of July 1763 till paid

WILLIAM HARRISON Plt. against JOHN ROBERTS & JONATHAN SMITH For Debt

This day came the aforesaid Deft. and says that he cannot deny the writing obligatory in the Declaration mentioned nor but he he owes the said Plaintiff the sum of five pounds six shillings like as the Plaintiff against him complains, and its considered by the Court that the Plaintif recover of the said Defendant the aforesaid sum of five pounds six shillings as also his costs by him in this behalf expended

This Judgment except the costs is to be discharged on the payment of two pounds thirteen shillings current money with Lawfull Interest thereon after the rate of 5 per cent per annum from the thirteenth day of November 1756 till paid

Page 89. Caroline County Court 13th April 1764

ROBERT ROBERTS Plt. against WILLIAM BRAWHILL Deft. On Petition

The Plaintiff appearing & proving his demand Judgment is granted the Plt against the said Defendant for the sum of one pound Seventeen shillings current money with costs

The Inventory and appraisement of the Estate of THOS. FORTUNE deceased was returned and admitted to record

ROBERT ROBERTS against JOHN PICKETT JUNR. Deft. On Petition

This Suit is dismissed

GEORGE MADDISON Plt. Against JOHN PICKETT JUNR. Deft. Trespass Assault & Battery. The Defendant being thrice solemnly called and failing to answer Judgment is granted the Plaintif against the sd Defendt. for his costs in and about the said Suit expended

JUDITH HACKLEY Plt. against HAY TALIAFERRO Deft. In Debt
This suit is dismissed being agreed

FREDERICK FORSUN Plt. against JAMES FARISH Deft.
The Plantiff appearing and proving his demand Judgment is granted the Plaintiff for the sum of Two pounds & one shilling currt. money which he is ordered to pay unto the Plt with an Attorneys fee and costs, etc.

Page 90. Caroline County Court 13th April 1764

SAMUEL PEARSON Plt. against THOMAS BOOTH Deft. Case
The Defendant being solemnly called and failing to appear Judgment is granted the Plt against the said Defendant for the sum of Eleven pounds Ten shillings and three pence current money which he is ordered to pay unto the said Plaintif and also his costs by him in this behalf expended

SUSANAH COCKRAN Plt. against WILLIAM STEVENS Deft. Trespass, Assault and Battery. And now at this day came the parties aforesaid by their Attorneys and thereupon came also a jury to wit JAMES LINDSEY etc being impanelled and sworn well and truly to try the matter in issue joind who having heard the arguments and evidences on both sides withdrew and in a short time returned the following Verdict. We of the Jury find for the Plaintif twenty shillings damages JAMES LINDSEY Foreman which Verdict at the Plaintifs motion is recorded & therefore its considered by the Court that the Plaintiff recover of the said Defendant the aforesaid sum of money by the Jurors in their Verdict aforesaid assest and also his costs by him for this behalf expended and the Deft. be in mercy etc.

JAMES MILLER Plt. against WILLIAM KING Deft. Trespass on the case
Now at this day came the parties aforesaid by their Attorneys & thereupon came also a Jury to wit JOSEPH TANKERSLEY etc being impannelled and sworn well and truly to try the matter

Page 91. Caroline County Court 13th April 1764

in Issue joined who having heard the arguments and evidences of each party withdrew and in a short time returned the following Verdict. We the Jury find for the Plaintif six pounds eleven shillings Current money. JOSEPH TANKERSLEY Foreman which Verdict at the Plaintifs motion is recorded Whereupon its considered by the Court that the Plaintif recover of the aforesaid Deft. the aforesaid sum of money by the Jurors in their Verdict assest and also his costs by him in this behalf expended & the sd Defendt. in mercy etc.

MATTHIAS ABBOTT Plt. against JOHN GODBY Deft. Trespass on the case
And now at this day came the parties aforesaid and thereupon also came a Jury to wit AQUILLA JOHNSTON etc. being impannelled and sworn well and truly to try the matter in issue joined who having heard the arguments and evidence of each party withdrew and in a short time returned the following Verdict. We of the Jury do find for the Plaintif five pounds current money which Verdict at the Plts. motion is recorded Therefore its considered by the Court that the Plaintif recover of the said Defendant the aforesaid sum of money by the Jurors in their Verdict aforesaid assest and also his costs by him in this behalf expended (and the Defendant be in mercy etc)

MARY CATLETT Plt. Against DUNCAN SANDEMAN Deft. Detinue

And now at this day came the parties aforesaid by their Attorneys & thereupon came also a Jury to wit JAMES LINDSEY etc. being impannelled & sworn

Page 92. Caroline County Court 13th April 1764

well and truly to trie the matter in Issue Joind and having heard the arguments and evidences on both sides withdrew and in a short time returned the following Verdict. We of the Jury find for the Plaintif the horse in the declaration mentioned of the price of six pounds current money and one penny damages JAMES LINDSEY foreman which Verdict at the Plaintifs motion is recorded and its considered by the Court that the Plaintif recover against the said Defendant the aforesaid sum of money by the Jurrors aforesd assest and also her costs by him in this behalf expended & the sd Deft. be in mercy etc.

JOHN SEMPLE Executor etc. of OBADIAH MARRIOTT deceased Plt
against ROBERT HUDGINS Deft.

The Plaintif having proved his demand Judgment is granted the Plaintif against the said Defendant for the sum of one pounds ten shillings six pence current money which he is ordered to pay unto the said Plaintiff with costs etc and the Sherif having made return thereof that he attachd. in the hands of ROBERT TALIAFERRO its therefore ordered that he cause the said attachd. goods to be sold and the money arising from the sale to go in satisfaction of the debt and costs aforesaid

Memorandum the Plaintiff agrees to stay Execution two months

ANDREW COCKRAN & COMPY Plt. against JOHN JONES Deft. In Debt

Judgment is granted the Plaintiff against the said Defendant for his costs by him in this behalf expended etc.

Page 93. Caroline County Court 13th April 1764

CHARLES CRENSHAW Plt. against JAMES HURT Deft. Debt

This suit is dismissed

REUBEN TURNER Plt. against GEORGE WILY Deft. Debt

And now at this day came the aforesaid Defendant and says that he cannot deny the writing obligatory in the declaration mentioned nor but he owes the said Plantif the sum of Ten pounds like as the Plt. against him complains Whereupon its considered by the Court that the Plaintif recover of the aforesaid Defendant the aforesaid sum of money and also his costs by him in this behalf expended.

This Judgment except the costs is to be discharged on the Defendants paying five pounds four shillings and eleven pence current money with Interest thereon from the 1st day of May 1763 till paid staying execution till June next

FRANCIS COLEMAN Plt. against GEORGE GOBORN Deft. Debt

Judgment is granted the Plt against the said Deft. for his costs by him in this behalf expended

ARCHIBALD GOWAN Plt. against THOMAS COLEMAN Deft. On Petition

The Plaintif appearing and proving his account, Judgment is granted the Plt agst the said Defendant for the sum of two pounds three shillings and five pence current money which he is ordered to pay unto the Plaintif with an Attorneys fee and cost

Page 94. Caroline County Court 13th April 1764

Its ordered that MARY CATLETT pay (   ) DOGETT three hundred seventy five pounds of Tobacco for fifteen days attendance as an evidence for her against SANDEMAN

Its ordered MARY CATLETT pay GILES NEWTON five hundred & twenty five pounds of tobacco for five days attendance as an evidence for her against SANDEMAN

THOMAS BRIDGFORTH Plt. against FRANCIS THORPE Deft. Trespass on the Case By consent of parties and by the Order of Caroline County Court this suit is referred to SIMON MILLER & JOHN ROWZEE and their award being returned as follows. We the subscribers have settled the accounts between the aforesd parties and we do award that the Plaintif recover against the said Defendant the sum of Eight pounds Fourteen shillings current money. Given under our hands this 11th day of Febry. 1764. SIMON MILLER, JOHN ROWZEE. And its ordered by the Court that the plaintiff recover of the said Defendant the said sum of money and also his costs by him in this behalf expended

Its ordered SUSANAH COCKRAN pay WILLIAM WOOD one hundred pounds of Tobacco for one days attendance and once coming and returning twenty five miles as an evidence for her against STEVENS.

Its ordered FREDERICK FORSON pay JOSEPH TANKERSLEY one hundred and fifty pounds of Tobacco for six days attendance as an Evidence for him against FARISH.

Page 95. Caroline County Court 13th April 1764

WILLIAM RITCHESON Plaintiff against JOSEPH DEJARNETT & NATHANIEL RITCHESON Deft. In Debt. This day came the aforesaid Defendants in their proper person and says that they cannot deny the writing obligatory in the declaration aforesaid alledged nor but they owe the said Plaintif the sum of nine pounds thirteen shillings like as the said Plaintif for his declaration aforesaid against him complains Therefore it is considered by the Court that the Plaintif recover against the said Defendt. the aforesaid sum of money as also his costs by him in this behalf expended

This Judgment (except the costs) is to be discharged on the Defendants paying four pounds sixteen shillings and six pence Current money with lawfull Interest thereon from the first day of March 1762 till paid Stayg. Exec. 3 month

WILLIAM RITCHESON Plaintiff against JOSEPH DEJARNETT & WILLIAM BOWLER Defts. In Debt. And now on this day came the aforesaid Defts. and says that they cannot deny the writing obligatory in the Plaintifs Declaration aforesaid alledged nor but they owe the said Plt the sum of Twelve pounds like as the Plaintif in his declaration aforesaid against him complains, Therefore its considered by the Court that the Plaintif recover against the said Defts. the aforesaid sum of money & also their costs by them in this behalf expenced

This Judgment (except the costs) is to be discharged on the Defendants paying six pounds current money with Interest thereon from the first day of March 1763 till paid Stayg. Exec. 3 months

Page 96. Caroline County Court 13th April 1764

NICHOLAS MULLIN Plt. against MORDECAI ABRAHAM Deft. In Case

And now on this day came the aforesaid parties by their Attorneys and thereupon came also a Jury (to wit) JAMES LINDSEY etc. being elected tryed and sworn the truth to speak upon the Issue Joined, and having heard the arguments and eveidences on both sides withdrew and in a short time returned the following verdict. We of the Jury find for the Defendant JAMES LINDSAY foreman which verdict on the Defendants motion is recorded,Whereupon its considered by the Court that the Plaintif take nothing by his Bill but for his false clamour be in mercy etc. that the said Defendant go thereof without day and recover of the sd Plaintif his costs by him about his defence in his behalf expended and the Plaintif may be taken etc.

Its ordered that NICHOLAS MULLIN pay JAMES BOWLWARE one hundred & seventy five pounds of Tobacco for seven days attendance as an evidence for him against MORDECAI ABRAHAM.

Its ordered that NICHOLAS MULLIN pay MARY BOULWARE one hundred and fifty pounds of Tobacco for six days attendance as an evidence for him against MORDECAI ABRAHAM.

Its ordered that MATTHEW ABBOTT pay JAMES DABNEY nine hundred & twenty pounds of Tobacco for fourteen days attendance and ten times coming and returning nineteen miles out of HANOVER as an evidence for him against GODBY.

Ordered MATTHEW ABBOTT pay JOHN BUTLER three hundred & twenty five pounds of Tobacco for 13 days attendance as an evidence for him against GODBY

Page 97. Caroline County Court 13th April 1764

Its ordered MORDECAI ABRAHAM pay SARAH MUNDAY one hundred and fifty poundsof Tobacco for 6 days attn. as an evidence for him at the suit of NICHOLAS MULLIN.

Its ordered NICHOLAS MULLIN pay JANE WATSON one hundred pounds of tobacco for four days attendance as an evidence for him against MORDECAI ABRAHAM

Its ordered MORDECAI ABRAHAM pay ANN FROMAGE one hundred and fifty pounds of Tobacco for six days attendance as an evidence for him at the suit of NICHOLAS MULLIN.

Ordered MORDECAI ABRAM pay SARAH ABRAM one hundred and fifty pounds of Tobacco for six days attendance as an evidence for him in the suit against NICHOLAS MULLIN

Ordered that MORDECAI ABRAHAM pay DARKUS MURRAY fifty pounds of Tobacco for two days attendance as an evidence for him at the Suit of NICHOLAS MULLINS

In the Petition brought by JOHN and WILLIAM McCALLs Plt. against JOHN PAGE Defendant Judgment is granted the Plaintif against the sd Defendant for his costs by him in this behalf expended

In the Petition brought by RICHARD JOHNSTON and JOHN BOSWELL Merchants & Partners Plantifs against JAMES HURT Defendant the said Plaintifs appearing and proving their demand, Judgment is granted them against the sd Defendant for the sum of three pounds and seven pence current money which he is ordered to pay unto the sd Plaintifs with an Attorneys fee and costs

Page 98. Caroline County Court 13th April 1764

JOHN BROADDUS Plt. against RICHARD FORTUNE Deft. On Petition
Judgment is granted the Plaintif against the said Defendant in the sum of one pound sixteen shillings and four pence current money with Interest thereon from the twenty second day of October 1762 till paid which he is ordered to pay the said Plaintif with costs etc.

FRANCIS TAYLOR Gent. Plt. against THOMAS BOOTH Gent.Deft. In Debt
Judgment is granted the Plt against the said Defendant for his costs by him in this behalf expended

JOHN WAGGENOR Plt. against JOHN PITTS and THOS. HEATH Defts. Debt
This is dismissed as to PITTS. And on the part of the said HEATH he appeared waved his plea and Confest Judgment for the sum of twenty six pounds five Shillings and ten

pence current money ballance of a note in hand which he is ordered to pay unto the sd Plaintif with costs etc.

For the Scire Facias sued out by WILLIAM LYNE Plaintiff to renew a Judgmt. of this County Court granted him against FRANCIS FLEMING & Wife the 18th day of August 1762 for twelve pounds eight shillings and eight pence current money and fifteen shillings or one hundred and fifty pounds of Tobo. for an Atts. Fee and two hundred and twenty seven pounds of Tobo. for cost of the Suit and the said Defendant having waved his plea its considered by the Court that the Judgment be renewed the Plaintiff to be paid the aforesd

Page 99. Caroline County Court 13th April 1764

sum of money and that he may have execution for the same with costs.

WM. RENOLDS Plt. against WILLIAM BOWLER Deft. In Debt

This day came the aforesaid Defendant and says that he cannot deny the writing obligatory in the Plaintifs declaration aforesaid alledged nor but he owes the said Plainfif the sum of Seventy four pounds Eighteen shillings like as the said Plaintif in declaration aforesaid against him complains, Therefore it is considered by the Court that the Plaintif recover of the aforesaid WILLIAM BOWLER the aforesaid sum of money and also his costs by him in this behalf expended

This Judgment (except the costs) is to be discharged on the Defendant & his Security paying the sum of Thirty seven pounds nine shillings current money with lawfull Interest thereon after the rate of five per cent per annum from the fifteenth day of April 1761 till paid, Staying Execution three months

SAMUEL HARTGROVE & THOS. TERRELL Exrs. of HENRY TERRELL deced Plt. against WILLIAM BOWLER & ROBERT MICKLEBURROUGH Defts. Debt

And now at this day came the aforesaid Defts. in their proper person & says they cannot deny the writing obligatory in the Plts. Declaration mentioned nor but that they owes the said Plts. the sum of thirty six pounds sixteen shillings two pence like as the said Plts. against them complain, Therefore it is considered by the Court that the Plaintifs recover against the said Defts. and ROBERT MICKLEBURROUGH his security the aforesaid sum of money as also their costs by them in this behalf expended.

This Judgment (except the costs) is to be discharged on the

Page 99a. Caroline County Court 13th April 1764

Defendant and his security paying the sum of Eighteen pounds eight Shills. and one penny Current money with Interest thereon from the 12th day of August 1762, Stayg. Execution three months

JOHN CARTER JUNR. Plt. against ROBERT RENNOLDS Deft. Case

This suit is dismissed

DOCTER WILLIAM JOHNSTON Plt. against GRIFFIN CARTER Deft. On Petition

This suit is dismissed

ELIZABETH CHARLES Widow Plt. against JAMES CHARLES Deft. Trespass Assault & Battery. This suit is dismissed being agreed

JAMES BOWIE Assee. of THOMAS COGHILL Plt. against BERNARD GAINS and JAMES GOUGE Deft. In Debt Judgment is granted the Plaintif against the said Defendant for his costs by him in this behalf expended

Its ordered that SUSANAH COCKERAN pay AQUILLA JOHNSTON two hundred and fifty pounds of Tobacco for two days attendance as an evidence for her against STEVENS

RICHARD DURRETT Plt. against ROBERT JOHNSTON JUNR. Deft. On an Attachment This suit is dismissed

Page 100. Caroline County Court 13th April 1764

ROBERT ROBERTS Plt. against NICHOLAS MULLIN Deft. On Petition The Plaintif having proved his demand Judgment is granted him against the said Defendant for the sum of one pound six shillings and six pence half penny current money which he is ordered to pay the said Plaintif with costs etc.

ROBERT ROBERTS Plt. against FRANCIS FLEMING Defendant On Petition The Plaintif having proved his account, Judgment is granted him against the Defendant for two pounds eight shillings and eight pence current money and also his costs by him in this behalf expended

ROBERT ROBERTS Plt. against WILLIAM HARPER Deft. On Petition This suit is dismissed

ELIZABETH HARRISON Plt. against FRANCIS PICKETT Deft. On Petition This suit is dismissed

ROBERT ROBERTS Plt. against BENJAMIN MAY Defend. On Petition Dismissed

MOSES HIGGINBOTTOM Plt. against WILLIAM GRAVES Deft. Case Judgt. is granted the Plt. agst the sd Deft. for his costs by him in this behalf expended

Page 101. Caroline County Court 13th April 1764

BENJAMIN RENNOLDS Plaintiff against JAMES DISMUKES Defendant On a Petition This suit is dismissed

Its ordered that the Churchwardens of Dysdale Parish bind out JOHN SIMMONS and HENRY JOHN, SIMON SMALL according to law it appearing to the Court that their Parents did not take proper care of them

ALEXANDER ATCHISON Plaintiff against WILLIAM BOWEN Defendant On Petition The Plaintiff having proved his demand, Judgment is granted him against the said Defendant for three pounds Current and also his costs by him in this behalf expended

JOHN TAYLOR Gent. Plaintif against JOHN PETROSS Defendant On an Attachment The Defendant being thrice Solemnly called and failing to appear Judgment is granted the Plaintif against the said Defendant in the sum of one pounds thirteen shillings and eight pence current money which he is ordered to pay unto the sd Plaintif and also his costs by him in this behalf expended

And the Sherif having made return thereof that he attached in the hands of JAMES TAYLOR Plt. and the said Garnishee appearing declares he has in his hand of the said Defendant the sum of three pounds current money and its ordered that the Garnishee deliver up the same to the Sherif & the said Sherif satisfy the Judgment therewith and render the surplus to the Defendant

Page 102. Caroline County Court 13th April 1764

JOHN SHIRLEY Plaintif against WILLIAM BROWN Deft. On Petition The Plaintif haveing proved his demand, Judgment is granted him against the said Defendant for two pounds fifteen shillings current money which he is ordered to pay unto the said Plaintif with an Attorneys Fee and cost

JOHN TAYLOR Merchant Plaintif against JOHN WILY Defendant Trespass on the Case. Now at this day came the parties aforesaid by their attorneys and mutually agreed to wave the Issue to the Countrey and submit the matter to the Judgment of the Court. Whereupon all and singular the premises being seen and by the Court fully understood its considered that the Plaintif recover against the said Defendant the sum of Sixty five pounds current money and also his costs by him in this behalf expended

JOHN TAYLOR Plaintiff against THOMAS COLEMAN and GEORGE WILY Defendts. Trespass in the Case. Now this day came the parties aforesaid by their Attorneys who mutually agreed to wave the Issue to the Countrey and submit the matter to the Judgment of the Court Whereupon all and singular the premises being seen and by the Court fully understood, its ordered that the Plaintif recover against the said Defendant the sum of twenty one pounds eight shillings and two pence current money and also his costs by him in this behalf expended Staying Execution two months

HUGH LENOX Plaintif against WILLIAM BURDETT Deft. On Petition This Suit is dismissed

Page 103. Caroline County Court 13th April 1764

ALEXANDER BAINE Plaintif against AMBROSE ARNOLD Defendant In Debt This suit is dismissed

ROBERT FLEMING Plaintif against AMBROSE ARNOLD Defendant Trespass on the Case. This Suit is dismissed

ALEXANDER BAINE Plaintif against JOHN WIATT Defendant In Debt Judgment is granted the Plaintif agst the said Defendant for his costs by him in this behalf expended

WILLIAM OLIVER JUNIOR Plt. against JOHN DOWNER SENIOR Defendt. On a Petition Judgment is granted the Plaintif against the said Defendant for one pound ten shillings current money and fifty eight pounds of Neatt Tobacco also 1/6 for an Attorneys fee according to a former Judgment which he is ordered to pay unto the said Plaintif with an Attorneys fee and costs

JOHN SHIRLEY Plaintif against JAMES FARISH Defendt. On Petition The Plaintif appearing and proving his demand, Judgment is granted him against the said Defendant in the sum of one pound ten shillings current money which he is ordered to pay the said Plaintif with an Attorneys fee and costs

JOHN TAYLOR Plaintiff against WILLIAM TURNER Defendt. On Petition The Defendant confest Judgment to the Plt for two pound four shillings & ten pence half penny Currt. money which he is ordered to pay the Plt. with costs etc.

Page 104. Caroline County Court 13th April 1764

JOHN RICHARDS Gent. Plaintif against THOMAS RIDDLE JUNIOR Defendant On Petition. This suit is dismissed

JOHN TAYLOR Gent Plaintif against BATESWORTH GRASTY Defendant On a Petition The Plaintiff appearing and proving his demand, Judgment is granted him against the said Defendant in the sum of one pound five shillings & seven pence half penny Current money and also his costs by him in this behalf expended

BENJAMIN HUBBARD Gent. Plaintif against MUSE TAYLOR and JOHN CHENALT Defts. Detinue. This suit is dismissed

JURY SMITH Plaintif against JAMES HURT Defendant Trespass This suit is dismissed

ARON GENTRY Plaintif against THOMAS PRICE Defendt. Debt This suit is dismissed

In the Scire Facias sued out by PETER COPELAND Gent to renew a Judgmt. of this County Court granted him against JOHN MITCHELL 13 day of August 1762 for the sum of five pounds seven shillings & ten pence current money fifteen shillings or one hundred and fifty pounds of Tobo for an attorneys fee and one hundred and fifty pounds of Tobo for costs of the sd suit and the said Defendant having waved his Plea its considered

Page 105. Caroline County Court 13th April 1764

by the Court that the Judgment be renewed unto the said Plaintif for the sum of money aforesaid and that he may have Exc. for the same & costs etc.

THOMAS LOYDE Plaintif against ROBERT GARROTT Defendant On a Petition
The Plaintif on proving his demand, Judgt. is granted him against the said Defendt. and for a watch the value of five pounds current money which he is ordered to pay unto the said Plt with an attorney fee & costs etc.

JAMES GOUGE Plaintif against THOMAS ROYSTON Deft. On a Petition
Judgment is granted the Plaintif against the sd Defendant for the sum of three pounds sixteen shilling & four pence and also the costs by him in this behalf expended
This Judgment (except the Costs) is to be discharged on the Defendants paying one pound eighteen shillings and two pence current money with Lawfull interest thereon at the rate of five per cent per annum from the (blank) day of October 1763 till paid

JOHN TAYLOR Gent Plt. against JOHN FURGUSON Defendant Debt
This day came the aforesaid Defendant & says he cannot deny the writing obligatory in the Plaintifs declaration alledged but he owes the said Plaintif the sum of seven pounds nine shillings and nine pence like as the said Plaintif in his declaration aforesaid against him maintains Therefore its considered by the Court that the Plaintif recover against the said Defendt. the aforesaid sum of money & also his costs by him in this behalf expended

Page 106. Caroline County Court 13th April 1764

This Judgment (except the costs) is to be discharged on the Defendants paying three pounds fourteen shillings and ten pence current money with Interest thereon from the 23rd day of March 1763 till paid

JAMES STEWART Plaintiff against WILLIAM BOWLER Defendant Debt
This day came the aforesaid Defendant & says that he cannot deny the writing obligatory in the Plaintifs declaration mentioned nor but he owes the said Plt the sum of Thirty two pounds current money like as the said Plaintif in his declaration against him complains Whereupon it is considered by the Court that the Plaintif recover against the said Defendant the aforesaid sum of money and also his costs by him in this behalf expended
This Judgment (except the costs) is to be discharged by the Defts. paying sixteen pounds current money with interest thereon from the 10 day of Apl. 1762 till paid, Staying Execu. three months
And the Sherif having returned an attachment that he attached the Estate one bed and furniture its therefore ordered that the Sherif sell the same according to law and the money arising from the sd sale to go in satisfaction of the Plaintifs Judgment and costs abovesaid & make report etc.

JAMES GOUGE Plaintif against JOHN FERGUSON Defendant On a Petition
Judgment is granted the Plaintiff against the aforesaid Defendant for the sum of three pounds fourteen shillings and ten pence and also his costs by him him in this behalf expended. This Judgment (except the costs) is to be discharged on the Defendants

paying one pounds Seventeen shillings & five pence currt. money with Interest thereon from the 9 day of July 1760 till paid

Page 107. Caroline County Court 13th April 1764

WILLIAM RITCHESON Plaintiff against JEREMIAH RAWLINGS and WILLIAM BOWLER Defts. Debt. Now at this day came the aforesaid Defendants and says that they cannot deny the writing Obligatory in the Plaintifs declaration mentioned nor but they owe the said Plaintiff the sum of Twenty pounds like as the sd Plaintif is his declaration aforesaid against them complains, Therefore its considered by the Court that the Plaintif recover agst the said Defendant the aforesaid Sum of money and also his cost by them in this behalf expended

This Judgment (except the costs) is to be discharged on the Defendants paying eight pounds ten shillings and seven pence current money with Interest thereon from the 1st day of March 1762 till paid, Staying Execution three months

PETER HOW Esqr. Plaintif against WILLIAM CLATTERBUCK. Trespass on the Case This suit is dismissed

GEORGE STUBBLEFIELD Plaintif against RICHARD GOODALL Defendant Debt This suit is dismissed being agreed

RICHARD GOODALL Plaintif against GEORGE STUBBLEFIELD Defendant Debt This suit is dismissed on the Defendant paying costs.

Page 108. Caroline County Court 13th April 1764

WILLIAM JOHNSTON Plaintif against JOHN PETROSS Defendant Debt This suit is dismissed

THOMAS BURK Plaintif against JOHN SOUTHWORTH Deft. Debt Judgment is granted the Plaintif against the said Defendant for his costs by him in this behalf expended

ISABELLA ARNOLD Plaintif against JOHN BENGER Defendant On a Petition This suit is dismissed

RICHARD TUNSTALL Plaintif against JEREMIAH JORDAN Defendant On an Attachment The Defendant being thrice solemnly called and failing to appear, Judgment is granted the Plaintif against the said Defendant for thirteen pound eight shillings and ten pence current money which he is ordered to pay unto the Plaintif with lawfull interest thereon after the rate of five percent per annum from the Seventeenth day of June 1763 till paid and also his costs by him in this behalf expended

And the Sherif haveing made return on the said Attachment that he attached the Defendts. Estate a parcell of Tobacco not Stripd, three iron pots, one stone jug, one chest, one cowhide & a few other trifling things in the hands of JOHN ALMAND and he is ordered the sd Garnishee deliver the same to the Sherif and the said Sherif to sell the same according to law and the money arising from the sd Sale

Page 109. Caroline County Court 13th April 1764

to go in satisfaction of the Plaintifs Judgment etc.

WILLIAM BAKER Plaintif against JOHN BILLUPS Defendant On Petition This suit is dismissed

ARMISTEAD CHURCHELL Exor. etc of ARMISTEAD CHURCHELL deced Plt. against JOHN MILLER SENIOR Defendant On Petition

Judgment is granted the Plaintif against the said Defendant for the sum of Two pounds Seventeen shillings current money which he is ordered to pay the said plaintif with an atto. fee and costs

THOMAS PICKETT Plaintif against BENJAMIN LONG Defendant Attachment This suit is dismissed

WILLIAM SPILLER Plaintif against JOSEPH PRICE Defendant On Petition The Plaintif proving his demand Judgment is granted against the sd Defendant for the sum of one pound Eight shillings and Eight pence farthing current money which he is ordered to pay unto the said Plaintif with an attorneys fee and costs

Its ordered that FREDERICK FORSON pay JAMES DISMUKES JUNR. one hundred and fifty pounds of Tobo. for six days attendance as an evidence for him against FARISH

Page 110. Caroline County Court 13th April 1764

RICHARD JONES Plaintif against JOHN SUTTON Gent. Defendt. On motion Judgment is granted the Plt against the said Defendant for the sum of Fifty seven pounds eighteen Shillings and four pence current money according to an execution granted the Plaintiff against JOHN and GEORGE WILY as also fifteen shillings or one hundred and fifty pounds of Tobacco for Lawyers fee and one hundred and forty seven pounds of neat Tobacco which he is ordered to pay unto the said plaintif with costs This Judgment except the costs is to be discharged on the Defendants paying the sum of twenty eight pounds nineteen and two pence current money with lawfull interest thereon from the 9th day of September 1762 till paid

ROBERT GILCHRIST Plt. against BENJAMIN GRUBS & THOMAS SULLENGER Deft. Attachment. THOMAS SULLENGER by a note from under his hand confess Judgment to the Plaintif for the sum of one pound fourteen shillings and seven pence half penny current money which he is ordered to pay unto the Plt. with costs etc.

GEORGE SIMPSON Administrator etc. Plt. against JAMES HILL Defendant Debt Judgment is granted the plaintif against the Deft for his costs by him in this behalf expended

Page 111. Caroline County Court 13th April 1764

JOHN BOWLER Plaintiff against JOHN SUTTON Late High Sherif Defendant On Motion. Judgment is granted the Plaintif against the said Defendant for the sum of seventeen pounds current money and fifteen shillings or one hundred and fifty pounds of Tobacco for an attorneys fee and one hundred and forty seven pounds of Neat Tobo according to an execution granted the plaintif against JOHN WILY which he is ordered to pay the said Plt with costs etc.

This Judgment except the costs is to be discharged on payment of eight pounds ten shillings current money with Interest thereon from the 12 day of January 1760 till paid

JOHN BOWLER Plt. against JOHN SUTTON Gent. Deft. On motion Judgment is granted the Plt against the said Defendant for the sum of twenty nine pounds one shilling current money according to an execution granted the plaintif against JOHN WILY also fifteen shillings or one hundred and fifty pounds of Tobo. for an attorneys fee and one hundred and forty seven pounds of Tobo which he is ordered to pay unto the Plaintif with costs etc.

This Judgment except the costs is to be discharged on the payment of Fourteen pounds two shillings currt. money with Lawfull interest thereon from the 25th day of December 1759 till paid

Page 112. Caroline County Court 13th April 1764

MATTHIAS GALE Merchant Plaintif against HARRY BEVERLEY Defendant Case And now at this day came the aforesaid parties by their attorneys who mututally agreed to wave the Issue to the Countrey and Submit the matter to the Judgment of the Court, Whereupon all and Singular the premises being seen and by the Court fully understood, its considered that the Plaintif recover against the aforesaid Defendant the sum of Ten pounds fourteen Shillings and six pence Sterling which he is ordered to pay unto the Plaintif with costs etc. and the Defendant be in Mercy etc.

This Judgment may be discharged in current money at the rate of fifty two percent for the difference of exchange

THOMAS DIXON Plaintif against BENJAMIN HUBBARD Deft. Debt

The Defendant being thrice Solemnly called and failing to appear Judgment is granted the Plaintif against the said Defendant for the sum of Twelve pounds eighteen shillings & nine pence Sterling with Interest thereon after the rate of ten per cent from the twenty sixth day of July 1762 till this July and five per cent till paid and also costs by him in this behalf expended

This Judgment is to be discharged in currt. money at the rate

Pages 113-116 are missing. The next page shows at the top May 1764 and appears to be a continuation of Grand Jury presentments. (Page 117 is partially missing)

Page 117. Caroline County May Court 1764

We do present JOHN ELLIOT PAINE in Drisdale Parish for not frequenting his Parish Church according to law.

We do present JOHN PANELL (?) in Drisdale Parish for not frequenting his Parish Church according to law.

We do present THADDEUS PANELL(?) in Drisdale Parish for not frequenting his Parish Church according to law

We do present ROBERT JORDAN in Drisdale Parish for not frequenting his Parish Church according to law

We do present EASTER BELL of St. Marys Parish for not giving a list of her land according to law

And its ordered the several Offenders be summoned to the next Court to answer this presentment

The Grand Inquest against CHRISTOPHER ( ), SIMON MILLER. HENRY BUCK-HANNON, ROBERT BEVERLY, CHARLES WALDEN, DAVID STERN, BARNARD MOORE, ( ) GILLISON and EASTER BELL is dismissed they paying ( )

EDMUND TAYLOR his Deed ( ) to JOHN TAYLOR Gent was proved by the oaths of the Witnesses and admitted to record

An assignment and power of attorney from FRANCIS FLEMING to EDMUND PEN-DELTON Gent was acknoweldged by the said FRANCIS and admitted to record

PATRICK COCKERAM is appointed Overseer of the road in the room of DAVID STERN

FREDERICK FORSON Plt. against JAMES (This entry is torn out)

Page 118. Caroline County May Court

Its ordered FREDERICK FORSON pay BENHAMIN BAUGHAN one hundred and seventy pounds of Tobacco for seven days attendance as an evidence for him against

JAMES GEORGE

ROBINSON DANGERFIELD Plaintif against JAMES POWELL Defendant On Petition Judgment is granted the plaintif against the said Defendant in the sum of two pounds shillings and eight pence which he is ordered to pay unto the said plaintif with an Attorneys fee & costs

This Judgment except the costs is to be discharged on the Defendant paying the sum of one pound three thillings and four pence current money with Lawfull Interest thereon from the Twelfth day of May one thousand seven hundred and sixty three till paid

CHARLES PORTER Plaintif against WILLIAM BOWLER Defendant On Petition Judgment is granted the plt against the said Defendant for the sum of three pounds current money which he is ordered to pay unto the said Plaintif with an Attorneys fee and costs.

FRANCIS FLEMING acknowledged his Declaration to EDMUND PENDLETON gent and its ordered to be recorded

Present ROBERT GILCHRIST Gent

The Inventory and apparisement of the Estate of GEORGE ROBINSON deceased was returned and admitted to record

Page 119. Caroline County May Court 1764

ROBERT GILCHRIST Gent is appointed to take the list of tithables in Saint Marys Parish

ANTHONY THORNTON Gent is appointed to take the list of tithables in the upper part of Drisdale and WILLIAM PARKER in the lower part and WILLIAM TYLER in the upper part of St. Margaretts and JOHN BAYNHAM in the lower parts

Its ordered that WILLIAM TYLER, ROBERT TALIAFERRO, AQUILLA JOHNSON or any two of them agree with workmen to rebuild TARPLAINS BRIDGE, and the DOGE TOWN BRIDGE

EDWARD STANLEY Power of Attorney to EDWARD DIXON was proved by the Oaths of JAMES BOWIE and ROBERT GILCHRIST Gent witnesses thereto and admitted to record

Its ordered that JOHN SNEED and HUGH CROUTCHER with their gangs open the Road from the Creek to the THREE NOTCHED ROAD by ROBERT CHEWNINGs and make report of their proceedings to Court

Its ordered that JOHN BROADDUS, RICHARD SNEED and WILLIAM MOTHLEY with their gangs open the road from the Glebe to the THREE NOTCHED ROAD by Mrs. FOSTERs and make report

Its ordered that THOMAS DUDLEY and THOMAS HEATH with their gangs open the Road from the Glebe to COLONEL BAYLORs and CHARLES BEASLEY and CHARLES BEASLEY JUNIOR their hands be joined to DUDLEYs and HEATHs gangs and make report

A Deed from JOHN MILLER and SUSAN his Wife to SIMON MILLER was proved by the Oaths of the witnesses and admitted to record

JOHN BROADDUS Plt. against JOHN THOMAS Deft. In Debt
The Defendant being thrice solemnly called and failing to appear the former order of Last November Court is confirmed against him for the sum of sixty five pounds Eleven shillings and one pence half penny and also his costs by him in

Page 120 Caroline County May Court 1764

this behalf expended therefore its considered by the Court that the Plaintif recover against the said Deft. the aforesaid Debt and Damages and the said Defendant in mercy etc. This Judgment except the costs to be discharged on the Defendants paying the sum of thirty pounds four shillings Eleven pence farthing current money with Interest on thirty two pounds six shillings and one penny farthing part thereof from the twenty third day of July one thousand seven hundred and sixty three till paid

THOMAS ELLIOT Plaintif against THOMAS BURK Defendant Trespass on the Case This suit is dismissed

ANDREW COCHRAN etc. Plt. against JAMES LINCH Deft In Debt

The Defendant being thrice solemnly called came not Judgment is granted the Plaintif against the said Defendant in the sum of Forty four pounds ten shillings and nine pence current money which he is ordered to pay unto the said plaintif and also the costs by him in this behalf expended

This Judgment except the cost is to be discharged on the Defendant paying the sum of twenty two pounds five shillings and four pence half penny current money with Lawfull interest thereon from the ninth day of March one thousand seven hundred and sixty three till paid - Staying execution three months

JOHN RICHARDS Plaintif against ABRAM Heree(?) In Debt

The Defendant by note from under his hand confest Judgment to the said Plaintif for the sum of twenty five pounds Eleven shillings and nine pence current money therefore its ordered that the Plaintif recover of the aforesaid Defendt. the aforesaid sum of money and also his costs by him in this behalf expended

Page 121. Caroline County May Court 1764

This Judgment except the cost is to be discharged on the Defendants paying the sum of twelve pounds seven shillings and ten pence half penny current money with Interest thereon from the 1st day of July one thousand seven hundred and sixty three till paid

FRANCIS COLEMAN Plaintif against CHARLES CULLIN Defendant In Debt

The Defendant by note from under his hand confest Judgment unto the said Plaintif for the sum of eighteen pounds current money therefore its ordered by the Court that the Plaintif recover against the aforesaid Defendant the said sum of eighteen pounds and also his costs by him in this behalf expended

This Judgment except the costs to be discharged by the Defendant paying the sum of nine pounds current money with lawfull Interest thereon from the Sixth day of March one thousand seven hundred and sixty three till paid

FRANCIS COLEMAN Plaintif against WILLIAM SAMUEL Defendant In Debt

The Defendant being three times called and came not, the former order of last November Court is confirmed against him for the sum of twenty pounds current money therefore its considered by the Court that the Plaintif recover against the said Defendant the aforesaid sum of twenty pounds and also his costs by him in this behalf expended

This Judgment except the costs is to be discharged by the Defendants paying the sum of ten pounds current money with Lawfull Interest thereon from the sixth day of May one thousand seven hundred and sixty three till paid

Page 122. Caroline County May Court 1764

WILLIAM WOODFORD gent against WILLIAM BOWLER gent Defendant On Petition

Judgment is granted the Plaintif against the said Defendant for the sum of three pounds one shilling and three pence current money which he is ordered to pay unto the said Plaintif with costs etc.

JOSEPH GATEWOOD Plaintif against JAMES GATEWOOD Defendt. On Petition This Suit is dismissed

Messrs. JOHNSTON & BOSWELL Plt against AMBROSE ARNOLD On Petition This suit is dismissed

WILLIAM EUBANKs Deed indented to BENJAMIN TEMPLE was proved by the Oaths of two of the witnesses and ordered to be certified

JANE CHALMERS and SARAH CHALMERS being this day admitted to choose a guardian makes choice of BENJAMIN HUBBARD Gent which was approved of by the Court and the said HUBBARD acknowledged a bond for the same

GEORGE PEARY acknowledged his Bill of Sale to ARCHIBALD ( ) which was admitted to record

Page 123. Caroline County May Court 1764

JAMES MILLER Plaintif against JACOB LOVELL Defendant In Debt
The Defendant by a note from under his hand confest Judgment to the said Plaintif in the sum of sixteen pounds ten shillings and ten pence current money with Interest on the same from the twentififth day of March one thousand seven hundred and sixty two till paid, therefore it is considered by the Court that the Plaintif recover against the said Defendant the aforesaid sum of money and Interest on the same as aforesaid and also his costs by him in this behalf expended

FRANCIS TAYLOR Gent Plaintif against JOHN WILY Defendant and GEORGE WILY In Debt The Defendant being three times called and failing to appear the former order of last November Court is confirmed against him for the sum of nineteen pounds one shilling and six pence current money, therefore its considered by the Court that the plaintif recover against the aforesaid Deft. the aforesaid sum of money and also his costs by him in this behalf expended.
This Judgment except the costs is to be discharged upon the Defendants paying the sum of nine pounds ten shills. and nine pence current money with lawfull Interest thereon from the first day of October one thousand seven hundred and sixty three till paid

The Inventory and appraisement of the Estate of JOHN CASON deceased was this day returned and admitted to record

Page 124. Caroline County May Court 1764

JAMES MILLS plaintif against WILLIAM BOWLER and JOSEPH DEJARNETT Defendants Debt The Defendants failing to appear on the plaintifs motion an Attachment is awarded him against the Estate of the said Defts. and the Sherif haveing made return thereof that he attached of the Defts. Estate one feather bed and furniture whereupon Judgment is granted the Plaintif against the said Defendants for the sum of thirty two pounds which he is ordered to pay unto the said Plaintif with costs which he hath sustained in this behalf expended. And Its ordered that the Sherif cause the said goods to be sold and the money arising from the said Sale to go in Satisfaction of the Debt and costs afsd.
This Judgment except the cost is to be discharged on the Defendants paying the sum of sixteen pounds current money with lawfull interest thereon from the Seventh day of March one thousand seven hundred and sixty three till paid

HUGH LENOX Plaintif against RICHARD McKENDRY Defent. In Debt
This suit is dimsissed

ROBERT FARISH and ANN his Wife she being first privately examined acknowledged their Deed Indented to JOHN JOHNSTON and its admitted to record

WILLIAM GOODALL is appointed Overseer of the Road in the room of JOHN THILMAN and its ordered that he keep the same in repair accordg. to law.

Page 125. Caroline County May Court 1764

JOHN MINOR is appointed overseer of the Road in the room of THOMAS CHEADLE deceased and its ordered that he keep the same in repare according to law

JOHN RICHARDS Plaintif against RICHARD RIDDLE Defendant In Debt
This day came the aforesaid Deft. and says that he cannot deny the writing Obligatory in the Plts. Declaration mentioned nor but he owes the said Plaintif the sum of Seven pounds eleven shillings and four pence like as the said Plt against him complains; therefore its considered by the Court that the Plaintif recover against the said Defendant the aforesaid sum of Money and also his costs by him in this behalf expended
This Judgment except the cost is to be discharged on the Defendants paying the full sum of five pounds fifteen shillings and eight pence current money with Interest from the sixteenth day of July one thousand seven hundred and sixty two till paid

ANDREW COCHRAN Plaintif against JOHN PETROSS Defendant In Debt
And now at this day came the aforesd Defendant and says that he cannot deny the writing Obligatory in the Plaintifs declaration aforesaid mentioned nor but that he owes the said Plaintif the full and just sum of thirty pounds nine shillings and two pence like as the said Plaintif in his Declaration aforesaid against him complains, its therefore considered by the Court that the Plaintif recover against the aforesaid Defendant the aforesaid Sum of money and also his costs by him in this behalf expended
This Judgment except the costs is to be discharged on payment of fifteen pounds four shills. Seven pence currt. money with Interest from the seventh day of December 1762 till paid

Page 126. Caroline County May Court 1764

ANDREW COCHRAN Plt. against JAMES FARISH Defendant On Petition
The Plaintif on proving his Demand Judgment is granted the Plaintif against the Defendt. for the sum of three pounds twelve shillings current money which he is ordered to pay unto the said Plaintif with costs

JOHN HOOMES Orphan of GEORGE HOOMES deceased comes this day admitted to choose a Guardian makes choice of EDMUND PENDLETON Gent who with JOHN BAYLER Gent his Security acknowledged bond for the same

BERNARD MOORE Plaintif against ROBERT MICKLELBERRY & THOMAS BANKS Defts. In Debt. And now this day came the aforesaid Defendants and says that they cannot deny the writing Obligatory in the Plaintifs declaration against them alledged nor but they owe the said Plaintif the full and just sum of one hundred and thirty five pounds current money like as the said Plaintif in his declaration aforesaid against them complains, its therefore considered by the Court that the Plaintif recover against the said Defendants the aforesaid Sum of one hundred & thirty five pounds current money and also his cost by him in this behalf expended
This Judgment except the cost is to be discharged in the Defendants paying the just sum of Fifty three pounds Six shillings and three pence half penny current money with lawfull Interest thereon from the Seventh day of July one thousand seven hundred and sixty two till paid.

Its Ordered that the Court be adjourned till tomorrow nine O'clock

RO: GILCHRIST

Page 127. Caroline County Court 11th day of May 1764

At a Court continued and held for Caroline County on ffriday the 11 day of May 1764

Present	ROBERT GILCHRIST,	ANTHONY THORNTON	)	
	WILLIAM TYLER	WILLIAM PARKER	)	his Majesties Justices
	JOHN TAYLOR	JAMES TAYLOR	)	
	JOHN BAYNHAM		)	

THOMAS PENNINGTON Plaintif against WILLIAM JOHNSTON JUNIOR Deft. In Debt This Suit is dismissed

CATHARINE MICOU Plaintif against ROBERT CALL Defendant On Petition This Suit abates by reason of the Defendants death

MAURICE KNIGHT Plaintif against MARK MARRIOT & JNO. MOTHLEY Defts. On Petition The Plaintif proving his demand Judgment is granted him against the aforesaid Defendants for the sum of two pounds fifteen shillings current money which they are ordered to pay unto the said Plaintif with costs

A Deed from JANE THILMAN and ELIZA. THILMAN to JNO. SUTTON was acknowledged by the said JANE and ordered to be recorded

Page 128. Caroline County Court 11th day of May 1764

ELIZABETH EMERSON Plaintif against WILLIAM McWILLIAMS Defendt. On Petition. The Plaintif appeared in open Court and proving her demand Judgment is granted her against the aforesaid Defendant for the just sum of Two pounds fourteen shillings current money and one hundred and eight pounds of tobacco which the Deft. is ordered to pay unto the said Plt. with costs

ELIZABETH EMERSON Plaintif against PATRICK CARY Defendant On Petition On the Plaintif appearing in open Court and proving her demand Judgment is granted her against the said Defendant for the sum of two pounds Seven shillings and six pence which he is ordered to pay unto the said Plaintif with costs

Its ordered that ELIZABETH EMERSON pay JOHN EMERSON two hundred and seventy five pounds of Tobacco for eleven days attendance as an Evidence for her against WILLIAM McWILLIAMS

FRANCIS FLEMING Plaintif against JOHN HERNDON Defendant On Petition This Suit is dismissed

Present JAMES JAMESON gent

Page 129. Caroline County Court 11th day of May 1764

ROBERT ROBERTS Plaintif against HARRY BEVERLEY Defendant On Petition Judgment is granted the Plt. against the said Defendant for his costs by him in this behalf expended

JAMES GARNETT Plaintiff against JAMES GOUGE Defendant In Debt Now at this day came the aforesaid Defendant and says he cannot deny the writing Obligatory in the plaintifs declaration against him alledged nor but he owes the said Plaintif the sum of Ninety two pounds eighteen shillings and six pence current money like as the said plaintif in his declaration aforesaid against him complains; therefore its considered by the Court that the Plaintif recover against the aforesaid Defendant the aforesaid sum of money and also his costs by him in this behalf expended

This Judgment except the cost is to be discharged on the payment of forty six pounds nine shillings and three pence current money with Interest thereon from the first day of October one thousand seven hundred and sixty two till paid

Present EDMUND PENDLETON Gent

An Indenture of Apprenticeship between WILLIAM WATERS and RICHARD BOULWARE was approved of by the Court and ackowledged by the parties and ordered to be recorded

Page 130. Caroline County Court 11th of May 1764

JOHN LEWIS Plaintif against JOHN ALMOND Defendant Trespass on the Case And now on this day came the aforesaid parties by their Attorneys and thereupon came a Jury to wit CHARLES STORY etc. were impannelled and sworn well and truly to try the matter in Issue Joined who having heard the arguments & evidence of each party withdrew and in a short time returned their Verdict in the following words (to wit) We of the Jury find for the Plaintif ten pounds ten shillings current money Damage CHARLES STORY foreman, which Verdict on the Plaintifs motion is recorded, and its therefore considered by the Court that the Plaintif recover against the said Defendant the aforesd sum of money by the Jurors in their Verdict aforesaid assessed and also his cost by him in this behalf expended and the sd Defendant in mercy etc.

JOHN TOWNSEND Plaintif against JOHN SUTTON Defendant In Trespass A Jury being impannelled & sworn well and truly to try the matter in Issue Joined by name CHARLES STORY etc. have heard the councill on both sides withdrew and was short time returned the following Verdict. We of the Jury do find for the Defendant CHARLES STORY foreman, which Verdict on the Defendants motion is recorded, therefore its considered by the Court that the Plaintif take nothing by his Bill but for his false clamour be in mercy; and the said Defendant go thereof without day and recover against the said Plaintif his cost by him about this defence in this behalf expended

Page 131. Caroline County Court 11th day of May 1764

THOMAS RENNOLDS Plaintif against RENNOLDS McKENNY Defendt. In Ejectment for 1000 acres of land of THOMAS RENNOLDS
This day came the aforesaid parties by their Attorneys and thereupon a Jury to wit JOHN ALMAND etc. being impannelled and sworn well and truly to try the matter in Issue joined and having heard the arguments and evidences of each partie withdrew and in a short time returned the following Verdict. We of the Jury find for the Defendant. JOHN ALMAND foreman, which Verdict on the motion of the said Defendant is recorded, its therefore considered by the Court that the plaintif take nothing by his Bill but for his false clamour be in mercy, and the said Deft. go thereof without day and recover against the said Plaintif his cost by him in this Defence in this behalf expended

THOMAS RENNOLDS Plaintiff against RENNOLDS McKENNY Defendant. Trespass Assault & Battery. And now this day came the aforesaid parties by their Attorneys and thereupon came also a Jury to wit JOHN ALMAND etc. being elected tried and sworn well and truly to trie the matter in Issue Joind and having heard the arguments and evidences on both sides withdrew and in a short time returned their Verdict; which Verdict in the following words to wit. We of the Jury do fine for the Plaintif one shilling damages. JOHN ALMAND foreman; which Verdict on the Plaintifs motion is recorded; its therefore considered by the Court that the Plaintif recover against the said Defendant the aforesaid sum of one shillings damage by the Jurors in their Verdict aforesaid assessed and also his costs by him in this behalf expended and the sd Defendant in mercy etc.

Page 132. Caroline County Court 11th day of May 1764

Its ordered that JOHN ALMAND pay JOSEPH WOOLFOLK one hundred and fifty pounds of Tobacco for six days attendance as an evidence for him agst. LEWIS

On the motion of JOHN RICE LOW an evidence for JOHN LEWIS against JOHN ALMAND its ordered that the said LEWIS pay him three hundred pounds of Tobacco for twelve days attendance. On the motion of JOHN PLANT an evidence for JOHN LEWIS against JOHN ALMAND he haveing attended twelve days its ordered that the said LEWIS pay him three hundred pounds of Tobacco for the same

On the motion of JOHN MARTIN an Evidence for JOHN ALMAND at the suit of JOHN LEWIS he haveing attended six days, its ordered that the said ALMAND pay him one hundred and fifty pounds of Tobacco for the same

On the motion of ROBERT MICKLEBERRY an Evidence for JOHN LEWIS against JOHN ALMAND he haveing attended ten days its therefore ordered that the said LEWIS pay him two hundred and fifty pounds of Tobo. for the same. This is not to be taxed in the Bill

On the motion of THOMAS JONES an Evidence for JOHN TOWNSEND against JOHN SUTTON he haveing attended six days its ordered that the said TOWNSEND pay him one hundred and fifty pounds of Tobacco for the same

On the motion of RICHARD EDMONDSON an Evidence for JOHN SUTTON at the suit of JOHN TOWNSEND he haveing attended ten days its ordered that the said SUTTON pay him two hundred and fifty pounds of Tobacco for the same

Page 133. Caroline County Court 11th day of May 1764

WILLIAM WILLSON Plaintif against AMBROSE FLETCHER Trespass of Assault and Battery. Now this day came the aforesaid parties by their Attorneys and thereupon came also a Jury to wit JOHN ALMAND etc who being elected tried and sworn the truth to speak upon the Issue joined and haveing heard the arguments and evidences of each partie; they withdrew and in a short time returned the following Verdict. We of the Jury fine for the Plaintif twenty pounds current money, which Verdict on the plaintifs motion is recorded, Therefore its considered by the Court that the plaintiff recover against the said Defendant the aforesaid sum of money by the Jurors in their Verdict aforesaid assest and also his costs by him in this behalf expended and the said Defendant in mercy etc

On the motion of EDWARD BRASFIELD an evidence for THOMAS RENNOLDS against RENNOLDS McKENNEY he haveing attended eleven days its ordered that the said RENNOLDS pay him two hundred and seventy five pounds of Tobacco for the same

On the motion of JOHN DOLLAR an evidence for THOMAS RENNOLDS against RENNOLDS McKENNEY he haveing attended twelve days its therefore ordered that the said RENNOLDS pay him three hundred pounds of Tobacco for the same

On the motion of JOHN TURNER an evidence for JOHN TOWSEND against JOHN SUTTON he haveing attended eight days its therefore ordered that the said TOWNSEND pay him two hundred pounds of Tobacco for the same

Page 134. Caroline County Court 11th day of May 1764

JOHN RENNOLDS Plaintif against JOHN PICKETT Defendant Slander

This day came the aforesaid parties by their Attorneys and there came a Jury to wit THOMAS JONES etc being impannelled sworn well and truly to try the matter in issue joined and they haveing heard the arguments and evidences of each partie withdrew and in a short time returned the following Verdict. We of the Jury fine for the Plaintif twenty five pounds current money THOMAS JONES foreman, which Verdict on the plaintifs motion is recorded, Therefore its considered by the Court that the Plaintif recover of the said Defendant the aforesaid sum of Money by the Jurors in their Verdict aforesaid and also his costs by him in this behalf expended & the said Defendant in mercy etc.

JOHN RENNOLDS Plaintif against JOHN PICKETT Defendant Trespass on the Case And Now at this day came the aforesd parties by their Attorneys and thereupon came also a Jury to wit CHARLES STORY etc who being elected tried and sworn the truth to speak upon the Issue Joined and haveing heard the arguments and evidences of each partie withdrew and in a short time returned the following Verdict. We the Jury fine for the Plaintif twenty five pounds current money damage CHARLES STORY foreman, which Verdict on the motion of the plaintif is recorded, Therefore its considered by the Court that the Plaintif recover against the said Defendant the aforesaid sum of money by the Jurors in their Verdict aforesaid assessed and also his costs by him in this behalf expended and the said Defendant be in mercy etc.

Page 135. Caroline County Court 11th day of May 1764

On the motion of SAMUEL NORMENT an evidence for JOHN TOWNSEND against JOHN SUTTON he haveing attended ten days its ordered that the said TOWNSEND pay him two hundred and fifty pounds of Tobacco for the same

On the motion of JAMES SOUTHWORTH an evidence for JOHN SUTTON in the suit of JOHN TOWNSEND, he haveing attended ten days, its ordered the said SUTTON pay him two hundred and fifty pounds of Tobacco for the same

On the motion of JANE NEILING an evidence for JOHN ALMAND at the suit of JOHN LEWIS and the said NEILING haveing attended four days its ordered that the said ALMAND pay her one hundred pounds of Tobacco for the same

On the motion of AARON QUESENBERRY an Evidence for RENNOLDS McKENNY at the suit of THOMAS RENNOLDS, he haveing attended ten days and hath come and returned thirty five miles seven times and its therefore ordered that the said McKENNY pay him nine hundred and eighty five pounds of tobacco for the same (ejectment suit)

On the motion of BENJAMIN JOHNSTON an evidence for RENNOLDS McKENNY at the suit of THOMAS RENNOLDS, and he haveing attended eleven days, its ordered that the said McKENNY pay him two hundred and seventy five pounds of Tobacco for the same in the ejectment suit

On the motion of THOMAS SHIP an evidence for THOMAS RENNOLDS against RENNOLDS McKENNY, he haveing attended ten days, its therefore ordered that the said RENNOLDS pay him two hundred and fifty pounds of Tobacco for the same

Page 136. Caroline County Court 11th day of May 1764

JEFFREY JUDGRIGHT Plaintif against VIOLENT VEXALL Defendt. (In margin: ROBINSON v BUCKNER) In Ejectment

for two Messuages or plantations and one thousand acres of land as also one messuage and Water Grist Mill with the appurtenances situate lying and being in the Parish of Drisdale and County of Caroline to have and to hold the said messuage, plantation, lands and Mill unto himthe said JEFFREY from the day next before the first day of September 1762 for and during the full term and time of seven years be fully completed and ended by virtue of which demise the sd JEFFREY afterwards to wit the same day and year afterwards entered in and upon the premises aforesaid and was thereof possessed untill afterwards to wit the same day and year aforesaid at the Parish and County aforesaid the sd Defendant with force of armes in and upon the possession of him the said Plaintif entered and he the said Plaintif from his farm in the premises aforesaid his term in the same still being to come and unexpired did violently expell and eject and other enormities to him the said Plaintif the sd Deft. then and there did and committed against the peace of our Lord the King his Crown and dignity and to the damage of the Plaintif forty pounds current money and therefore he brings suit

SEMPLE for the Plt

Mr. JOSIAS PLUNKETT and Mr. GRIFFIN JONES. You will see by the above declaration that I am ( ) for lands now in your possession you will therefore appear at the next court to be held for the said County on the second Thursday in next month and enter yourself Defendant in this Suit other waies I shall suffer Judgment to go against me by default

Page 137. Caroline County Court 11th day of May 1764

and you will turned out of possession I am your Humble Servant

VIOLENT VEXALL

To Mr. JOSIAH PLUNKETT and Mr. GRIFFIN JONES JUNR. in possession of the premises or some part thereof on the (blank) day of (blank) one thousand seven hundred and (blank) the within JOSIAS PLUNKETT and GRIFFIN JONES JR.with a true copy of the within declaration and endorsements thereon upon the lands within mentioned

WILLIAM HARRISON

And now at this day to wit At a Court held for the said County of Caroline this twelfth day of May 1763 Appearing by the affidavit of WILLIAM HARRISON that JOSIAS PLUNKETT and GRIFFIN JONES Tenants in possession of part of the premises in the Declaration mentioned hath been Legally served with a true copy of the Declaration and endorsements thereon its ordered that unless the said JOSIAS PLUNKETT and GRIFFIN JONES or they under whom they claim haveing legal notice of this order appear at the next Court to be held for the County and make themselves Defendants in this fact and without delay plead not guilty enter into the common rule for ( ) Lease entry and agree to ( ) on the title only at trial that Judgment be entered for the Plaintif by default and his Majesties Writ of habere facias possessionem ( ) And at this day to wit at a Court held for the same county on the (blurred) day of September 1763 On the motion of SAMUEL BUCKNER and MARY his Wife, BAWLDWIN MATHEWS BUCKNER and JOHN BUCKNER they are admitted Defendants in this Case in the room of the said VIOLENT VEXALL and having confest the Lease entry in the Declaration supposed and agreed to insist on the title only at trial by (blank) the matter in this fact pleaded not guilty of the trespass and ejectment in the Declaration supposed and of this the Plantif Joined the issue

Page 138. Caroline County Court 11th day of May 1764

tendered, therefore the Sherif is commanded that he cause to come here at the next Court to be held for this County twelve by whom and who either to recognize a Verdict because the same day is given to the said parties here and at this day to wit at a Court held for the said County on the Seventh day of May 1764 came the aforesaid parties by their Attorneys and thereupon all and Singular the premises being Seen and by the Court of our said Lord the King here fully understood upon mature deliberation thereof had for that it appears to the Court now here upon the whole matter that the Laws for the Plaintif therefore it is considered that he recover against the said Defendant his term yet for to come of and in the land and premises aforesaid with the appurtenances in the Declaration mentioned and its further considered that the Lessor of the Plaintif recover against the said Defendants BUCKNERS his costs by them in this behalf expended and the said Defendant may be taken etc. ( ) indicates words not read)

On the motion of ABRAHAM HARPER an evidence for JOHN PICKETT at the suit of JOHN RENNOLDS he haveing attended seven days its ordered that the said PICKETT pay him one hundred and seventy five pounds of Tobo for the same -- second suit

On the motion of JAMES RENNOLDS an evidence for JOHN RENNOLDS against PICKETT he haveing attended eleven days its ordered that he pay him two hundred and seventy five pounds of Tobo. for the same -- second suit

Page 139. Caroline County Court 11th day of May 1764

On the motion of THOMAS RENNOLDS an evidence for JOHN RENNOLDS against JOHN PICKETT he haveing attended ten days its ordered that the said RENNOLDS pay him two hundred and fifty pounds of Tobacco for the same -- in the second suit

On the motion of SARAH YOUNG an evidence for JOHN RENNOLDS against JOHN PICKETT she haveing attended ten days its ordered that the said RENNOLDS pay her two hundred and fifty pounds of Tobacco for the same -- in the second suit

EASTER BELL returns an account of two hundred and ninety two acres of land that she hath in Saint Marys Parish

JOHN BELL returns an account of one hundred and twenty eight acres of land which he ommitted giveing in last year

On the motion of JOHN CROUTCHER an evidence for JOHN RENNOLDS against JOHN PICKETT he haveing attended twelve days its ordered that he pay him three hundred pounds of Tobacco for the same

On the motion of WILLIAM HOARD an evidence for JOHN RENNOLDS against JOHN PICKETT he having attended twelve days its ordered that the said RENNOLDS pay him three hundred pounds of Tobacco for the same in the second suit

On the motion of BENJAMIN SNEED an evidence for JOHN RENNOLDS against JOHN PICKETT he haveing attended twelve days its ordered that the said RENNOLDS pay him three hundred pounds of tobacco for the same In the second suit

JOHN TAYLOR Plaintif against THOMAS JONES Defendant On an Attachment This Suit is dimissed

Page 140. Caroline County Court 11th day of May 1764

JOHN TAYLOR Plaintif against JOHN BRANGHILL (BRAWHILL in margin) Defendant. In Debt. And now at this day came the aforesaid Defendant by his Attorney and says that he cannot deny the writing Obligatory in the plaintifs Declaration mentioned nor but he owes the said Plaintif the sum of thirty five pounds Sixteen shillings like as the said Plaintif in his Declaration aforesaid against him complains, therefore its considered by the Court that the Plaintif recover against the said Defendant the aforesaid sum of money and also his cost by him in this behalf expended

This Judgment except the cost is to be discharged on the Defendants paying the sum of Seventeen pounds eighteen shillings current money with lawfull Interest thereon from the 23rd day of April 1763 till paid

BENJAMIN HUBBARD Plaintif against MOZA HURT Defendant On Attachment Judgment is granted the Plaintif against the said Defendant for the sum of ten pounds five shillings and eleven pence current money which he is ordered to pay unto the said Plaintif with costs etc.

And the Sherif having made return thereon that he executed the said Attachment in the hands of WILLIAM BOWLER gent and its ordered that the said BOWLER deliver the said attach'd goods to the Plaintif and Satisfy the Debt and costs aforesd and render the overplus if any to the Defendant and make report

Page 141. Caroline County Court 11th day of May 1764

JOHN TAYLOR Plaintif against GEORGE EVANS Defendant Trespass on the Case
This Suit is dismissed

JOHN TAYLOR Plaintif against GEORGE EVANS Defendant In Debt
This Suit is dismissed

JOHN PICKETT JUNR. Plaintif against BENJAMIN HUBBARD Defendt. Trespass on the Case. And Now this day came the said parties by their attorneys who mutually agreed to wave the issue to the Country and submit the matter to the Judgment of the Court whereupon all and singular the premises being seen and by the Court fully understood its considered that the Plaintif recover against the said Defendant the sum of fourteen pounds five shillings current money and also his cost by him in this behalf expended and the said Defendant in mercy Staying execution three months

On the motion of JOHN RENNOLDS an evidence for JOHN PICKETT against BENJAMIN HUBBARD he haveing attended eleven days and hath come and returned Sixteen miles seven times its therefore ordered that the said PICKETT pay him Six hundred and eleven pounds of Tobo. for the same

On the motion of WILLIAM BOWLER an evidence for BENJAMIN HUBBARD at the suit of JOHN PICKETT he haveing attended six days its ordered that the said HUBBARD pay him one hundred and fifty pounds of Tobacco for the same

Page 142. Caroline County Court 11th May 1764

On the motion of JAMES DISMUKES an evidence for JOHN PICKETT against BENJAMIN HUBBARD he haveing attended eleven days its therefore ordered that the said PICKETT pay him two hundred and seventy five pounds of Tobacco for the same

JAMES MILLS Plaintif against JOHN MILLS etc. Defendants In Debt
The Defendant appeared in open Court and confest Judgment unto the said Plaintif for the sum of one hundred and eighty pounds current money Therefore its ordered that the Plaintif recover against the sd Defendant the aforesaid sum of money and also his cost by him in this behalf expended

This Judgment except the cost is to be discharged on the Defts. paying the several and respective sums hereafter mentioned together with Interest as followeth that is to say fifteen pounds with Int. from the 6 day of September 1757 till paid and fifteen pounds with Interest from the 6 day of September 1758 till paid and Interest on fifteen pounds from the 6 day of Sept. 1759 and Interest on fifteen pounds from the 6th day of Sept. 1760 and Interest on fifteen pounds from the 6th day of Sept. 1761 and Interest on fifteen pounds from the 6 day of September 1762 till paid Staying execution 1 month

Its ordered that the Court be adjourned till tomorrow 9 O'Clock

Page 143. Caroline County Court 12th day of May 1764

At a Court continued and held for Caroline County on Saturday the 12 day of May 1764 Present EDMUND PENDLETON,)
ROBERT GILCHRIST) Gentlemen his Majesties Justices
JAMES JAMESON and)
JOHN TAYLOR)

JEREMIAH JORDANE Plaintif against JOHN WATTS Defendant Trespass on the Case
This Suit is Dismissed at the Plts. Cost

ANN JONES Plaintif against JEREMIAH SANDYS & JOHN TOWNSEND Defts. Debt
The Defendants being three times called and failing to appear the former order of last September Court is confirmed against them and MATHEW PETROSS there Security for the sum of Six pounds ten shillings current money with lawfull interest thereon from the first day of April one thousand seven hundred and sixty three till paid therefore its considered by the Court that the Plaintif recover against the said Defendants and Security the aforesaid sum of money and also his cost by him in this behalf expended

ELLIOTT EMERSON Plaintif against JOHN PICKETT JUNR. Defendant. Trespass of an Assault and Battery. This Suit is dismissed being agreed

Page 144. Caroline County Court 12th day of May 1764

THOMAS NORMENT Plaintif against JOHN GEORGE Defendant Debt
This suit is Discontinued

Present WILLIAM TYLER Gent

JOHN GRAHAM Plaintif against JOHN LONG Defendant In Debt
And now at this day came the aforesd Defendant and says that he cannot deny the writing Obligatory in the Plaintifs Declaration mentioned nor but he owes the said Plaintif the sum of fifty seven pounds and nine pence current money like as the said Plaintif against him complains, therefore its considered by the Court that the Plaintif recover against the aforesaid Deft. the sum of money and also their costs by him in this behalf expended

This Judgment except the cost is to be discharged on the Defendants paying the sum of twenty eight pounds ten shillings and four pence half penny current money with lawfull interest thereon from the Sixth day of September one thousand seven hundred and sixty two till paid

JOHN GRAHAM Plaintif against JOHN LONG Defendant Trespass on the Case
The Defendant appeared in open Court and confest Judgment to the Plaintif for ten pounds six shillings and five pence current money and its considered by the Court that the Plaintif recover against the said Defendant the aforesaid sum of money and also his cost by him in this behalf expended

Page 145. Caroline County Court 12th day of May 1764

JOHN GRAHAM Plaintif against JACOB LOVELL Defendant Debt
This suit is dismissed

WILLIAM JOHNSTON Plaintif against DANIEL McCOY Defendant In Debt
The Defendant being thrice times called and failing to appear, at the Plaintifs motion an attachment is awarded the Plaintif against the Estate of the said Defendant and the Sherif haveing made return thereof that he attached of the Defendants Estate one Sword whereupon Judgment is granted the Plaintif against the said Defendant for the sum of five pounds twelve shillings and six pence current money and its considered by the Court that the Plaintif recover against the aforesaid Defendant the aforesaid Sum of money and also his costs by him in this behalf expended

And its ordered that the Sherif sell the said Sword according to Law and the money arising from the said Sale to go in satisfaction of the Plaintifs Judgment aforesaid and make report and so forth

This Judgment except the cost is to be discharged on the Defts. paying the sum of two pounds sixteen shillings and three pence current money -- no interest

WILLIAM JOHNSTON Plaintif against WILLIAM POE Defendant Trespass on the Case. Judgt. is granted the Plaintif agst the Defendt. for his costs by him in this behalf expended

Page 146. Caroline County Court 12th day of May 1764

ANN JONES Plaintif against FRANCIS TAYLOR & NATHANIEL NORMENT Deft. In Debt. And Now at this day came the aforesaid Defendants and says that they cannot deny the writing Obligatory in the Plaintifs declaration against them alledged nor but they owe the said Plaintif the sum of one hundred pounds current money like as the said Plaintif in her Declaration aforesaid against them complains therefore its considered by the Court that the Plaintif recover against the said Defendant the aforesaid sum of money and also her costs by him in this behalf expended

This Judgment except the costs is to be discharged on the Defendants paying the full and just Sum of fifty pounds current money with Lawfull Interest thereon after the rate of five per cent per annum from the tenth day of June 1762 till paid Staying Execution three months

JOHN PAGE Plaintif against WILLIAM MOTHLEY Defendt. Trespass on the Case This suit is discontinued

THOMAS PICKETT Plaintif against JAMES GEORGE Defendant. Trespass of Assault and Battery. Judgment is granted the Plaintif against the said Defendant for his costs by him in this behalf expended

Page 147. Caroline County Court 12th day of May 1764

JOHN BROADDUS Plaintif against AMBROSE TOOMBS Defendant In Debt

The Defendant being thrice Solemnly called and came not, the former order of Last August is confirmed against him and WILLIAM TOOMBS his Security for the sum of twenty two pounds fifteen shilling and five pence current money, therefore its considered by the Court that the Plaintif recover of the aforesaid Defendants the aforesaid sum of money and also his costs in this behalf expended

This Judgment except the cost is to be discharged on the said Defendants paying the just sum of Eleven pounds seven shillings and eight pence three farthing with Interest thereon from the sixth day of May one thousand seven hundred and sixty three till paid

JOSEPH FHIPPO Assee of JOHN JONES Plaintif against JOHN WILY Defendant In Debt. And now at this day came the aforesaid parties by their attorneys and mutually agreed to wave the issue to the Countrey and Submit the matter to the Judgt. of the Court, Whereupon all and Singular the premises being seen and by the Court of our said Lord the King fully understood its therefore considered that the Plaintif recover against the said Defendant the sum of forty pounds current money and also his costs by him in this behalf expended

This Judgment except the cost is to be discharged on the Defendts. paying the sum of twenty pounds current money

Page 148. Caroline County Court 12th day of May 1764

WILLIAM DARNEL JUNR. Plaintif against JAMES TALIAFERRO and JOHN SAMUEL Defts. In Debt This day came the aforesaid parties by their attorneys and the said Defendant waved the issue joined in the suit and confest Judgment to the said Plt. in the sum of twenty four pounds current money and its considered by the Court that the Plaintif recover of the said Defendants the aforesaid sum of money and also his cost by him in this behalf expended

This Judgment except the cost is to be discharged on the said Defendants paying the sum of twelve pounds current money with Lawfull interest thereon from the first day of December one thouand seven hundred and sixty two till paid

JONATHAN SYDENHAM Plaintif against LUNSFORD LOMAX Gent Defendt. On a Scire Facias The Sherif haveing made return on the said Writ that he executed it according to Law upon which Judgment is granted the Plaintif against the said Defendant for thirty pounds fourteen shillings and eight pence Sterling it being the principal Interest and charges of a Protested Bill of Exchange, fifteen shillings or one hundred and fifty pounds of Tobacco for an Attorneys fee and one hundred and eight pounds of Tobacco for costs of said Suit therefore its considered by the Court that the Judgt. of July Court one thousand seven hundred and fifty eight renewed unto the said Plaintif for the aforesaid sum with Interest thereon after the rate of five per cent from this day till paid and also the cost by him in this behalf expended

This Judgt. may be settled in currency according to the rate of 60 per cent exchange

Page 149. Caroline County Court 12th day of May 1764

(first name blotted) assee of BENJA. RUCKER Plaintif against RICHARD FORTUNE Defendant In Debt. And now this day came the parties by their Attorneys and the said Defendant waved the issue joined in this Suit and confest Judgment unto the said Plaintif for the sum of ninety pounds current money therefore it is considered by the Court that the Plaintif recover of the said Defendant the aforesaid sum of money and also his cost by him in this behalf expended

This Judgment except the cost is to be discharged on the Defendants paying the sum of fourty five pounds current money with interest thereon from the first day of April one thousand seven hundred and sixty two till paid

PATRICK COUTTS Plaintif against JOHN THILMAN Defendant In Debt

This day came the aforesaid parties by their Attorneys and the said Defendant by his Attorney waved the issue joined in this Suit and confest Judgment to the said Plaintif for the sum of one hundred twenty eight pounds sixteen shillings current money its therefore considered by the Court that the Plaintif recover against the said Defendant the aforesaid sum of money and also his cost by him in this behalf expended

This Judgment except the cost is to be discharged on the Defendants paying the sum of sixty four pounds eight shillings with lawfull Interest thereon from the first day of November one thousand seven hundred and sixty one till paid

Page 150. Caroline County Court 12th day of May 1764

ANN JONES Administrator etc. Plaintif against GEORGE WILY Defendant Trespass on the Case. This day came the aforesd Defendant and says he cannot deny the account in the Plts. Declaration mentioned nor but he owes the said Plaintif the sum of fourteen pounds and two pence current money like as the said Plaintif in her Declaration aforesaid against him complains therefore its considered by the Court that the Plaintif recover from the said Defendant the aforesaid sum of money and also his cost by him in this behalf expended

ANDREW COCHRAN Plaintif against JOHN SOUTHWORTH Defendant Trespass on the Case. And now at this day came the aforesaid Defendt. by his Attorney and waved the issue joined in the said suit and confest Judgment to the plaintif for the sum of Eleven pounds sixteen shillings and nine pence current money, therefore its considered by the Court that the Plaintif recover against the said Defendant the aforesaid sum of money and also his cost by him in this behalf expended

STEPHEN STONE Plaintif against FRANCIS FLEMING & JOHN ELLIOT PAINE Defendt. In Debt. And now this day came the aforesaid parties by their Attorneys and the said Defendants waved the issue joined in this Suit and confest Judgment to the said Plaintif for seven hundred pounds of Tobacco and Cask therefore its considered by the Court that the Plaintif recover against the said Defendants the aforesd quantity of Tobacco and cask and also his cost by him in this behalf expended

Page 151. Caroline County Court 12th day of May 1764

Messrs. DUNLOP and CROSSE Plaintif against JOHN MORGAN Defendant. Trespass on the Case. On now at this day came the aforesaid parties by their Attorneys and thereupon a Jury to wit JAMES LINDSEY etc being impannelled and sworn well and truly to Inquire into Damages and having heard the arguments and evidence of each partie withdrew and in a short time returned the following Verdict. We of the Jury fine for the Plaintif Six pounds fourteen shillings & eight pence current money Damage JAMES LINDSEY foreman, which Verdict on the Plaintifs motion is recorded, its therefore considered by the Court that the plaintif recover against the said Defendant and GEORGE CHAPMAN, JAS. ANDERSON, WHITAKER CAMPBELL and RO. JOHNSTON his Sectys. the aforesaid sum of money by the Jurors in their Verdict aforesaid assessed and also his costs by him in this behalf expended and the sd Defendant in mercy etc.

CHARLES BURRAS Plaintif against WILLIAM TYLER Defendant In Debt This day came the aforesaid parties by their Attorneys and the said Defendant waved the issue joined in this suit and confest Judgment to the said Plaintif for the sum of two hundred and fifty pounds current money, its therefore considered by the Court that the Plaintif recover against the aforesaid Defendant the aforesaid sum of money but no cost in this behalf expended.

This Judgment is to be discharged on the Defendants paying the sum of (fifty crossed out, L 225 inserted) currt: money with Interest on L 50 part thereof from the tenth day of June one thousand seven hundred and sixty till paid and Interest on Seventy five pounds from the tenth day of June one thousand seven hundred and sixty one till paid

Page 152. Caroline County Court 12th day of May 1764

CHARLES CUNNINGHAM Plt. against THOMAS BOOTH Defendant. Trespass on the Case. And now at this day came the aforesaid parties by there Attorneys and the said Defendant waved the issue Joined in this Suit and confest Judgment to the said Plaintif for the sum of ten pounds eight shillings current money, its therefore considered by the Court that the Plaintif recover against the said Defendant the aforesaid sum of money and also his cost by him in this behalf expended

CHARLES CHEWNING Plaintif against CHRISTOPHER CURTIS Defendant Trespass on the Case. This suit abates the Deft. being dead

JOHN PICKETT SENR. Plaintif against JOHN RENNOLDS & SARAH YOUNG In Debt And now at this day came the aforesd parties by their Attorneys and thereupon a Jury to wit ANTHONY SAMUEL etc being impannelled and sworn well and truly to try the matter in Issue joined who having heard the arguments and evidences of each party withdrew and in a short time returned the following Verdict. We of the Jury fine for the Defendants ANTHONY SAMUEL foreman, which Verdict on the Defendants motion is recorded; its therefore considered by the Court that the Plaintif take nothing by his Bill but for his false Clamour be in mercy, and the said Defts. go thereof without day and recover against the said Plaintif his cost by him about this defence in this behalf expended

Page 153. Caroline County Court 12th May 1764

WILLIAM BOWLER Plaintif against JOHN ELLIOT PAINE Defendant In Debt And now at this day came the aforesaid parties by their Attorneys, and the said Defendant waved the issue joined in this Suit and confest Judgment to the said Plaintif for the sum of thirty six pounds current money, therefore it is considered by the Court that the Plaintif recover against the said Defendant the aforesaid sum of money and also his cost by him in this behalf expended.

This Judgment except the cost is to be discharged on the Defendants paying the sum of Eighteen pounds current money with Lawful Interest thereon from the fifteenth day of June 1760 till paid

WILLIAM TALIAFERRO Plaintif against JAMES MILLER Defendant Trespass on the Case. This suit abates the Plt. being dead

JAMES GOUGE Plaintif against DUNKIN SANDERS Defendant Trespass on the Case And now at this day came the aforesaid parties by their Attorneys and mutually agreed to wave the issue to the Countrey and Submit the matter to the Judgment of the Court Whereupon all and Singular the premises being seen and by the Court fully understood its considered that the Plaintif recover against the said Defendant the sum of Eight pounds two shillings current money and also his costs by him in this behalf expended and the Defendant in mercy etc.

Page 152a. Caroline County Court 12th day of May 1764

JOHN GRAY Plaintif against JOHN EMERSON Defendant Trespass on the Case And now at this day came the aforesaid parties by their Attorneys and thereupon a Jury to wit ANTHONY SAMUEL etc. being impannelled and Sworn well and truly to enquire into Damages and having heard the arguments and evidences of each partie withdrew and in a short time returned this following Verdict. We the Jury fine for the Plaintif Six pounds three shillings and four pence current money ANTHONY SAMUEL foreman; which Verdict on the Plaintifs motion is recorded; its therefore considered by the Court that the Plaintif recover against the said Defendant the aforesaid sum of money and also his cost by him in this behalf expended

JOHN BLAND Plaintif against WILLIAM BOWLER Deft. Case This day came the aforesaid parties by their Attorneys and thereupon a Jury to wit JAMES LINDSEY etc. being Impannelled and sworn well and truly to enquire into Damages and haveing heard the Arguments and evidences of each party withdrew and in a short time returned the following Verdict. We the Jury fine for the Plaintif one hundred and ten pounds fourteen shillings and ten pence Sterling. JAMES LINDSEY foreman; which Verdict on the Plaintifs motion is recorded; therefore its considered by the Court that the Plaintif recover against the said Defendant the aforesaid sum of money and also his cost by him in this behalf expended the Judgment to be settled in Currency at the rate of sixty per cent for the difference of exchange

Page 153a. Caroline County Court 12th day of May 1764

JOHN GRAY Plaintif against JAMES BOWLER SENR. Deft. Trespass on the Case A Jury being impannelled and Sworn ANTHONY SAMUEL by name well and truly to enquire into the Damages and haveing heard the arguments and evidences of each partie withdrew and in a short time returned the following Verdict. We the Jury fine for the Plaintif twelve pounds four shillings and one penny half penny current money ANTHONY SAMUEL foreman; which Verdict on the plaintifs motion is recorded; therefore its considered by the Court that the Plaintif recover against the aforesaid Defendant the aforesaid sum of money by the Jurors in their said Verdict aforesaid assessed and also his cost by him in this behalf expended and the said Defendant in mercy etc.

JOHN GRAY Plaintif against ROBERT TALIAFERRO SENR. Deft. Trespass on the Case. And now at this Day a Jury being impannelled and sworn by name ANTHONY SAMUEL etc. well and truly to enquire of Damages and haveing heard the evidences and arguments on both sides withdrew and in a short time returned the following Verdict. We the Jury fine for the Plaintif two pounds eleven shillings and five pence current money ANTHONY SAMUEL foreman; which Verdict on the Plaintifs motion is recorded; therefore its considered by the Court that the Plaintif recover against the said Defendant the aforesaid sum of money by the Jurors in their Verdict aforesaid assessed and also his cost by him in this behalf expended and the said Defendant in mercy etc.

Page 154. Caroline County Court 12th day of May 1764

WILLIAM SPILLER Plaintif against CHARLES CARTER Defendant Trespass on the Case And now at this day came the aforesd parties by their Attorneys and the said Defendant waved the issue joined in this Suit and confest Judgment to the Plaintif for the sum of Thirty six pounds seventeen shillings and eight pence current money; therefore its considered by the Court that the Plaintif recover of the said Defendant the aforesaid Sum of money and also his cost by him in this behalf expended

REUBEN BROWN Plaintiff against EDWARD POWERS Defendant Trespass on the Case. This Suit is Dismissed by the Plaintif

JOHN MILLER Plaintif against EDWARD POWERS Defendant In Trespass This day came the parties by their Attorneys and thereupon a Jury to wit JAMES LINDSEY etc. being Impannelled and Sworn well and truly to trie the matter in issue joined and haveing heard the arguments and evidences of each party upon their oaths do say that the Defendant is Guilty in manner and form as the Plaintif against him hath complained and they do assess the Plaintifs Damages by occasion thereof to five pounds current money besides his cost; therefore it is considered that the Plaintif recover against the said Defendant five pounds current money damages in form aforesaid assessed and also his cost by him in this behalf expended and the said Defendant in mercy etc.

Page 155. Caroline County Court 12th day of May 1764

On the motion of EDWARD VAWTERS an evidence for JOHN MILLER agst EDWARD POWERS he haveing attended five days its ordered that he pay him one hundred and twenty five pounds of tobacco for the same and 90 lbs of Tobo more for twice coming and returning fifteen miles out of ESSEX.

On the motion of JOHN ROBINSON an evidence for JOHN MILLER against POWERS he haveing attended three days its ordered that the sd MILLER pay him seventy five pounds of Tobacco for the same

On the motion of JOHN MELEAR an evidence for JOHN MILLER against POWERS he haveing attended two days its ordered that the said MILLER pay him fifty pounds of Tobacco for the same

On the motion of AMBROSE HOARD an evidence of JOHN MILLER against POWERS he haveing attended three days its ordered tht the sd MILLER pay him Seventy five pounds of Tobacco for the same

On the motion of PAUL THILMAN an evidence for JOHN LEWIS against JOHN ALMAND he having attended five days and hath come and returned twenty five miles twice out of HANOVER its ordered that the said LEWIS pay him two hundred and fifty pounds of Tobacco for the same

WILLIAM BOWLER Plaintif against JOHN BOWCOCK Defendant In Debt
This day came the aforesaid parties by their attorneys the said Defendt. waved the Issue joined in this suit, and confest Judgment for the full and just sum of Twenty five pounds two shillings and three pence current money with Interest from the thirtieth day of March one thousand seven hundred and sixty three till paid and its considered that the Plaintif recover against the said Defendant the aforesaid sum of money and Interest as aforesaid and also his cost by him in this behalf expended

Page 156. Caroline County Court 12th day of May 1764

JAMES BOWIE Plaintif against WILLIAM KING Defendant In Trespass
And now at this day came the aforesd parties by there Attorneys and thereupon a Jury to wit JAMES LINDSEY etc being impannelled and sworn well and truly to try the matter in issue joined and having heard the arguments and evidences on both sides, they upon their oaths do say that the said Defendant is Guilty in the manner and form as the Plaintif against him hath complained, and they do assess the Plaintifs Damages by occasion thereof to twenty shillings besides his cost; therefore it is considered that the Plaintif recover against the said Defendant the twenty shillings Damage in form aforesaid assessed and twenty shills. for his cost in this behalf expended and no more and the said Defendant may be taken etc

On the motion of WILLIAM HOARD an evidence for JOHN RENNOLDS at the Suit of PICKETT he haveing attended one day its ordered that he pay him twenty five pounds of Tobacco for the same

On the motion of THOMAS PICKETT an evidence for JOHN RENNOLDS at the suit of PICKETT he haveing attended one day its ordered that the sd RENNOLDS pay him twenty five pounds of Tobacco for the same

On the motion of THOMAS RENNOLDS an evidence for JNO. RENNOLDS agst PICKETT he haveing attended one day its ordered that he pay him twenty five pounds of tobacco for the same

ZACHARIAH TALIAFERRO Plaintif against CHARLES CARTER Deft. Trespass
This Suit abates the Deft being dead

Page 157. Caroline County Court 12th day of May 1764

LUCRETIA SALMON Plaintif against ROBERT FARISH Defendant Trespass of Assault and Battery. And now at this day came the aforesaid parties by their attorneys and thereupon a Jury to wit JOHN JONES etc. who being elected tried and sworn the truth to speak upon the Issue Joind and haveing heard the arguments and evidences on both sides withdrew and in a short time returned the following Verdict. We the Jury do find for the Defendant JOHN JONES foreman; which Verdict on the Defendants motion is admitted to record; whereupon its considered by the Court the the Plaintif take nothing by her Bill for her false Clamour be in mercy and the said Defendant go thereof without day and recover against the said Plaintif his costs by her about this case in this behalf expended and the sd Plaintif may be taken

ARCHIBALD McCALL Assee of RICHARD ROY Plaintif against JOHN WILY Defendant. In Debt This day came the aforesaid parties by their attorneys and the said Defendant waved the Issue Joined in this Suit and confest Judgment to the sd Plaintif for

the sum of ninety five pounds current money; therefore its considered by the Court that the Plaintif recover of the said Defendant the aforesaid sum of money and also his cost by him in this behalf expended
This Judgment except the cost is to be discharged by the Defendants paying the sum of Forty seven pounds ten shillings current money with Lawfull Interest from the fourteenth day of October one thousand seven hundred and sixty two till paid

Page 158. Caroline County Court 12th day of May 1764

ANDREW COCHRAN etc. Plaintif against CHARLES CARTER Esqr. Defendt. In Debt This day came the aforesaid parties by their attorney & the said Defendant waved the Issue Joind in this Suit and confest Judgment to the Plaintif for the sum of one hundred and sixty pounds current money therefore it is considered by the Court that the plaintif recover against the said Defendant the aforesaid Sum of money with Lawfull Interest thereon from the first day of June 1763 till paid

JOSHUA TRAYNHAM Plaintif against JOHN WILY Defendant Tresspass on the Case
And now at this day came the aforesaid parties by their attorneys and thereupon a Jury to wit THOMAS JONES etc who being impannelled and Sworn well and truly to try the matter in issue joind who haveing heard the arguments of each party withdrew and in a short time returned the following Verdict. We of the Jury do fine for the Plaintif ten pounds current money THOMAS JONES foreman; which Verdict on the Plaintifs motion is recorded; Whereupon its considered that the plaintif recover against the said Defendant the aforesaid sum of money by the Jurors in their Verdict aforesaid assessed and also his cost by him in this behalf expended and the sd Defendant may be taken etc

JACOB KING Plaintif against WILLIAM POE Defendt. Case
Upon the Defendants acknowledging in open Court that he does not remember that ever he called the Plaintif a Mullato or that he knows that he is one and on the Defendant paying cost this Suit is dismissed

Page 159. Caroline County Court 12th day of May 1764

THOMAS METCALF Executor etc. Plaintif against LUDWEL GRIMES Defendant In Debt. This day came the aforesaid parties by their Attorneys, and the said Defendant waved the Issue Joined in this Suit and confest Judgment to the Plaintif for the sum of twenty one pounds four shillings and five pence Sterling; therefore its considered by the Court that the Plaintif recover against the said Defendant the aforesaid sum of money with Interest thereon after the rate of ten percent from the eighth day of May 1760 till this day and five percent till paid and also his cost by him in this behalf expended. This Judgment may be discharged in Currency at the rate of Sixty percent for the difference of Exchange

JOHN GRAY Plaintif against FRANCIS and DAVID STERNS Defendt. In Debt
This day came the aforesaid parties by their Attorneys, and the said Defendants waved the Issue and confest to the Plaintif for the sum of forty one pounds Seven shillings and three pence; therefore its considered by the Court that the Plaintif recover agst. the said Defendants the aforesaid sum of money and also his costs by them in this behalf expended. This Judgment except the cost is to be discharged on the Defendants paying the sum of Twenty pounds thirteen shillings and seven pence half penny current money with Lawfull Interest thereon from the twenty fifth day of June one thousand seven hundred and fifty seven till paid

Its ordered the Court be adjourned till the Court in Course

EDMUND PENDLETON

Page 160. Caroline County Court 14th day of June 1764

At a Court held for Caroline County on Thursday the 14th day of June 1764
Present: ROBERT GILCHRIST)
WILLIAM TYLER)
JOHN TAYLOR and) Gent his Majesties Justices
JOHN BAYNHAM

An Indenture of Apprenticeship between HUMPHREY LUCAS and JOHN OVERSTREET was acknowledged by the parties approved of by the Court and ordered to be recorded

BENJAMIN TEMPLE acknowledged his Deed and Bond Indented to JOHN FULCHER was proved by the oaths of the witnesses and admitted to record

JOHN PICKETT and MARY his Wife she being first privately examined acknowledged their Deed Indented to JOHN SNEED and was on the part of two witnesses proved by the oaths of the witnesses and on their motion is recorded

A Relinquishment of Dower from MATTHEW DAVIS and ANN his Wife to MATTHEW PETROSS was proved on the Oath of two of the witnesses and admitted to record

Absent ROBERT GILCHRIST Gent

On the motion of JOSEPH McGEHEE he is exempted from paiment of Levies and taxes for JOHN McGEHEE his Son until he the said JOHN shall arive to the age of twenty one years

The Inventory and appraisement of the Estate of RICHARD CLATTERBURK deced was this day returned and admitted to record

Page 161. Caroline County Court 14th day of June 1764

On the motion of THOMAS HALEY he is exempted from paying County Levyes

On the motion of SETH THORNTON its agreable to the Court that he shall qualify as a Vestry Man in Saint Marys Parish

JOHN MITCHELL acknowledged his Deed Indented to SAMUEL HAWES which at his motion is ordered to be recorded

SAMUEL HAWES acknowledged his Deed Indented to PETER GOODWIN which said Deed on his motion is admitted to record

The Grand Inquest against PETER ROBINSON is dismissed

On the motion of FRANCES HALBERT, she is appointed Guardian to MARTHA, FRANCIS and JOEL HALBERT Orphans of JOEL HALBERT deced and the said FRANCES acknowledged a bond for the same

The several Inventories and appraisements of the Estate of NICHOLAS BATTAILE deceased was this day returned and admitted to record

The Last Will and Testament of JAMES SINGLETON deceased was presented in Court by MARY SINGLETON Executrix therein named and who made Oath thereto according to Law and being further proved by the oath of one of the witnesses thereto and was admitted to record and the sd Executrix performing what is usual in such cases, certificate is granted her for obtaining a probate thereof in due form and acknowledged a bond for the same, and the said Executrix came into Court and renounced all benefit and advantage whatsoever from the sd Will

Its ordered that WILLIAM TYLER, ROBERT TALIAFERRO and AQUILLA JOHNSTON or any two of them do lett the building of DOWNERS BRIDGE and also for repairing the Causway; JOHN WILY haveing failed to perform the same according to agreement

Page 162. Caroline County Court 14th day of June 1764

Its ordered that JAMES MASON, CHARLES MASON, RICHARD DAVENPORT and MELCHRIDECK BRANN or any three of them being first sworn before a Justice of the peace for the said County do appraise the Estate of JAMES SINGLETON deceased and make report of their proceedings to Court

WILLIAM DANIEL and ELIZABETH his Wife she being first privately examined acknowledged their Deeds Indented to THOMAS RENNOLDS and admitted to record

WILLIAM DANIEL and ELIZABETH his Wife she being first privately examined acknowledged their Deed Indented to WILLIAM BEASLEY and admitted to record

WILLIAM BEASLEY and ANN his Wife she being first privately examined acknowledged their Deed Indented to CHARLES BEASLEY JUNR. and it was admitted to record

On the motion of THOMAS SAMUEL he is appointed CONSTABLE in the room of PETER BULLARD

BENJAMIN NORMENT is appointed Overseer of the Road in the room of JAMES MULLIN and its ordered that he keep the same in repair according to Law

On the motion of STEPHEN LOWE an evidence for JOHN TAYLOR against JOHN ELLIOT PAINE he haveing attended eight days its ordered that the said TAYLOR pay him two hundred pounds of Tobo for the same

On the motion of JOHN BUTLER its ordered that ANN BUTLER be summoned to appear at the next Court if she will administer on the Estate of JAMES BUTLER deceased

An Indenture of Apprenticeship between JAMES FLETCHER and DAVID STERN was approved of by the Court acknowledged by the parties and admitted to record

Page 162a Caroline County Court 14th day of June 1764

On the motion of BENJAMIN REYNOLDS an evidence for CORNELIUS BEASLEY against McCOY he haveing attended seven days its ordered that the said BEASLEY pay him one hundred and seventy five pounds of Tobacco for the same

CHURCHELLS Exors Plaintifs against JOHN MILLER SENR.Defendt. On Petition Judgment is granted the Plaintifs against the said Defendant for the sum of four pounds which he is order to pay unto the said Plaintifs with an attorneys fee and half the costs

WILLIAM JOHNSTON Plaintif against JOHN WYNAL SANDERS Defendt. On a Petition. On the Plaintifs proving his demand Judgment is granted him against the said Defendt. for the sum of three pounds Eighteen shillings nine pence three farthings current money which he is ordered to pay unto the said Plaintif with costs

WILLIAM JOHNSTON Plaintif against THOMAS REYNOLDS Defendant On Petition The Plaintif having proved his demand Judgment is granted him against the said Defendt. for the sum of three pounds five shillings and eight pence current money which he is ordered to pay unto the said Plt with cost.

Page 163. Caroline County Court 14th day of June 1764

CHARLES GOODALL Plaintif against JOHN SUTTON Defendant Trespass on the Case This day the aforesaid Deft. by a note from under his hand confest Judgment to the said Plt. for the sum of five pounds two Shillings and ten pence current money; therefore its ordered by the Court that the Plaintif recover of the said Defendant the aforesd sum of money and also his cost by him in this behalf expended

JOHN JOHNSTON Plaintif against CHARLES PORTER and BENJAMIN JOHNSTON Defts. In Debt. Dismissed

WILLIAM JOHNSTON Plaintif against JOHN WOOLFOLK Defendant Trespass on the Case. This suit is dismissed being agreed

JAMES ELPHERSTON Plaintif against WILLIAM BOWLER Defendt. on a Scire Facias This suit is dismissed

JOHN CORRIE Plaintif against JOHN BOWIE and BENJA. GATEWOOD Defendt. Debt Judgment is granted the Plaintif against the said Defendant for his Tobo cost by him in this behalf expended

RACHEL BAUGHAN Plaintif v MARK CARRELL Defendt. On Trespass This suit is dismissed

Page 164. Caroline County Court 14th day of June 1764

HARRY TOMPKINS Plaintif against WILLIAM JOINER Defendant On an Attachment. This suit is dismissed

EDWARD BROWN Plaintif against JOHN VICE JUNR. Defendant On an Attachment This suit is dismissed

JOHN ALMAND Plaintif against ROBERT LANKFORD Defendt. On an Attachment This suit is dismissed

WILLIAM JOHNSTON Plaintif against JOHN BROWN Defendant On Petition The Plaintif having proved his demand Judgment is granted the Plaintif against the said Defendt. for the sum of two pounds and six pence current money which he is ordered to pay with cost

RICHARD TUNSTALL Plaintif against JOHN LEE Defendant On Petition The Plaintif having proved his demand Judgment is granted against the said Defendant for the sum of one pound fifteen shillings and nine pence half penny current money which he is ordered to pay unto the said Plt. with an Attorneys fee and cost

On the motion of JOHN ALMAND an Evidence for RICHARD TUNSTALL against JOHN LEE he haveing attended one day its ordered that the sd TUNSTALL pay him twenty five pounds of Tobacco for the same

Page 165. Caroline County Court 14th day of June 1764

MARMADUKE STANFIELD Plaintif against WILLIAM EMERSON Defendant On Petition. The Plaintif having proved his demand Judgment against the said Defendant for the sum of three pounds current money and his costs in this behalf expended

On the motion of CHRISTOPHER ACOFF an Evidence for MARMADUKE STANFIELD against WILLIAM EMERSON he haveing attended four days its ordered that the said STANFIELD pay him one hundred pounds Tobo for the same

JOHN ALMAND Plaintif against ANTHONY LOFON Defendant On an Attachment Judgment is granted the Plaintif against the said Defendant for his cost in this behalf expended

WILLIAM WHITLOCK Plaintif against GEORGE WILY Defendant On Motion Judgment is granted the Plaintif for the sum of Fifty pounds Current money and fifteen shillings or one hundred and fifty pounds Tobacco for an Attorneys fee and one hundred and fifty pounds of Tobo which is according to a former Judgment and execution granted the Plaintif against the sd Deft. Therefore its ordered by the Court that the Plaintif recover against the said Deft. the aforesaid Sum of Money and Tobo and also his cost by him in this behalf expended

Page 166. Caroline County Court 14th day of June 1764

This Judgment except the cost is to be discharged on the Defendt's paying the sum of thirteen pounds three shillings and two pence Currency and the aforesaid sum of Tobo with Interst on the said sum of money above mentioned from the 20th day of May 1762 till paid and the said Defendt. may be taken

ELIZABETH SIDNOR Plaintif against WILLIAM BOWLER & JEREMIAH RAWLINGS Defendant On Motion. Judgment is granted the Plaintif against the said Defendants for the sum of twenty four pounds fifteen shillings Current money and fifteen shillings or one hundred and fifty pounds of Tobacco for an attorneys fee and two hundred pounds of Neat Tobo according to a former Judgment and Exe. against the said Defendant Therefore its considered by the Court that the Plaintif recover of the said Defendants the aforementioned sum of money and Tobacco and also her costs by him in this behalf expended

This Judgment except the cost is to be discharged on the Defendants paying the full and just sum of Twelve pounds Seven shillings and six pence Current Money and the above mentioned Tobo. with Interest on the said last mentioned sum of money from the Second day of March 1764 till paid

Its Ordered that the Court be adjourned till tomorrow morning nine O'clock

ROBERT GILCHRIST

Page 167. Caroline County Court 15th day of June 1764

At a Court continued and held for Caroline County on ffriday 15 day of June 1764

Present ANTHONY THORNTON)
WILLIAM PARKER) Gent his Majesties Justices
JOHN TAYLOR and)
GABRIEL THROCKMORTON)

GEORGE THOMAS Plaintif against WILLIAM BOWLER Defendant In Debt

This day the aforesaid Defendt. by note from under his hand says that he cannot deny the writing Obligatory in the Plaintifs Declaration mentioned nor but he owes the said Plaintif the sum of twenty seven pounds nine shillings and five pence Current money like as the said Plaintif in his Declaration aforesaid against him complains therefore its considered by the Court that the Plaintif recover against the aforesaid Defendant the aforesaid Sum of money with Interest thereon from the tenth day of June one thousand seven hundred and sixty three till paid Staying Exe. till August

GEORGE THOMAS Plaintif against WILLIAM BOWLER Defendant In Debt

This day the aforesaid Defendt. by a note from under his hand confest Judgment unto the said Plt. for thirty five pounds current money therefore its considered by the Court that the Plaintif recover of the said Deft. the aforesaid sum of money and his costs in this suit by him expended Staying Exe. till August

Page 168. Caroline County Court 15th day of June 1764

GEORGE THOMAS Plaintif against WILLIAM BOWLER Defendt. In Debt

This day came the Defendant by a note from under his hand and says that he cannot deny the writing Obligatory of the promisory note in the Plaintifs declaration mentioned; nor but he owes the said Plaintif the sum of fifteen pounds Current money like as the said Plaintif in his declaration aforesaid against him complains; therefore its considered by the Court that the Plaintif recover the aforesaid sum of money and also his costs by him in this behalf expended Stg. Exe. till August

HENRY GILBERT Plaintif against WILLIAM BOWLER & JOHN WIATT Defts. On Petition. Judgment is granted the Plaintif against the said Defendants for the sum of two pounds nine shillings and six pence Current money which he is ordered to pay unto the said Plaintif with an attorneys fee and cost

This Judgment except the cost is to be discharged on the Defents. paying the sum of one pound four shillings and nine pence Current money with Interest thereon from the first day of April 1763 till paid

SAMUEL PEARSON Plaintif against WILLIAM BOWLER Defendant On Petition Judgment is granted the Plaintif against the said Defendant for the sum of one pound thirteen shillings Current money and an attorneys fee and cost

Page 169. Caroline County Court 15th day of June 1764

CHRISTOPHER DICKEN Plaintif against JOHN NEWTON Defendant On Petition This Suit is dismissed

ROBERT TERRELL Plaintif against JOHN THILMAN Defendant On Petition The Plaintif on proveing his demand, Judgment is granted him against the said Defendant for the sum of two pounds twelve shillings and six pence Current money which he is ordered to pay unto the said Plt. with an attorneys fee and costs

On the motion of WILLIAM JOHNSTON its ordered his ORDINARY Licence be renewed he having acknowledged with sufficient security for the same

FRASER and STRAUGHAN Plaintif against PATRICK CARY On Petition This suit is dismissed

RICHARD TUNSTALL Plaintif against THOMAS BURTON Defendant On Petition Judgment is granted the Plaintif against the said Defendant for the sum of two pounds Current money with Interest thereon from the 3 day of September 1763 till paid which he is ordered to pay with an attorneys fee and cost

Page 170. Caroline County Court 15th day of June 1764

JOHN CORRIE Plaintif against JOHN BOWCOCK Defendant On Petition On the Plaintifs proveing his Demand Judgment is granted him against the said Defendant for the sum of two pounds five shillings and two pence Current money which he is ordered to pay unto the said Plaintif with an attorneys fee and cost

ARCHIBALD RITCHIE Plaintif against SAMUEL NORMENT Defendant On Petition On the Plaintifs proveing his demand Judgment is granted him against the said Defendant for the sum of one pound Seven shillings and one penny Currt. money which he is ordered to pay unto the said Plaintif with an attorneys fee and cost

DEKAR TOMPSON Plaintif against WILLIAM ROBINSON Defendant Trespass on the Case. Judgment is granted the Plt. against the said Defendant for his cost by him in this behalf expended

JACOB BURRIS Plaintif against JOHN WINAL SANDERS Deft. On an Attachment This suit is dismissed

THO. KING Plaintif against LAWRENCE ANDERSON Defendt. Presentment This is dismissed

Page 171. Caroline County Court 15th day of June 1764

JAMES TAYLOR gent Treasurer Plaintif against JOHN SUTTON gent late high Sheriff Defendt. On Motion. On this motion there is a Judgment granted the Plaintif against the said Defendt. for the sum of one hundred and sixteen pounds sixteen shillings and six pence current money therefore its considered that the Plaintif recover against the aforesaid Defendant the aforesaid sum of money and also his cost by him in this behalf expended and the said Defendant may be taken

ROBERT GILCHRIST gent Plaintif against JOHN MORGAN Defendant In Debt This Suit is dismissed

ROBERT GILCHRIST gent Plaintif against JOHN SELLS Defendant Trespass on the Case. This suit is dismissed

ROBERT GILCHRIST gent Plaintif against RICHARD MAJOR Defendant Trespass on the Case. This Suit is dismissed being agreed

ROBERT GILCHRIST gent Plaintif against WILLIAM WHITEHEAD Defendant Trespass on the Case. This suit is dismissed

Page 172. Caroline County Court 15th day of June 1764

LENOX SCOTT etc Plaintifs against ROGER GAINES Defendant On Petition This suit is dismissed

ALEXANDER ATCHISON Plaintif against JOHN TOWNSEND JUNIOR Defendt. On Petition Judgment is granted against the Defendant for the sum of two pounds current money which he is ordered to pay unto the said Plaintif with cost

WILLIAM BUCKNER Plaintif against PATRICK CARY Defendant. Trespass on the Case. This suit is dismissed

WILLIAM HARRISON Plaintif against BENJAMIN LONG Defendant. On an Attachment. This suit is dismissed

JAMES GOUGE Plaintif against LAWRENCE TALIAFERRO Defendant On Petition The Plaintif haveing proved his demand, Judgment is granted him against the said Defendant for the sum of one pound seventeen shillings and nine pence which he is ordered to (pay) unto the said Plaintif with cost

On the motion of PEYTON STERN an evidence for JAMES GOUGE against LAWRENCE TALIAFERRO he haveing attended seven days its ordered that the said GOUGE pay him one hundred and seventy five pounds of Tobo for the same

Page 173. Caroline County Court 15th day of June 1764

THOMAS PICKETT Plaintif against PETER BULLARD Defendant On Petition The Plaintif haveing proved his demand, Judgment is granted the Plaintif against the said Defendant for the sum of two pounds current money which he is ordered to pay unto the said Plaintif with costs

On the motion of PHILIP MAY an evidence for THOMAS PICKETT against PETER BULLARD he haveing attended five days its ordered the said THOMAS pay him one hundred and twenty five pounds of Tobacco for the same

WILLIAM JOHNSTON Plaintif against WILLIAM GOODALL Defendant On Petition The Plaintif haveing proved his demand, Judgment is gratned him against the said Defendant for the sum of two pounds two shillings and five pence one farthing current money which he is ordered to pay unto the said Plt. with cost

BENJAMIN ALSOP Plaintif against GEORGE CATLETT Defendant On Petition The Plaintif haveing proved his demand Judgment is granted him against the said Deft. for the sum of three pounds fifteen shillings & Eleven pence current money which he is ordered to pay unto the said Plt. with cost

Page 174. Caroline County Court 15th day of June 1764

DUNCAN GRAHAM Plaintif against WILLIAM BOWLER Defendant On a Protested Bill of Exchange. This day came the aforesaid Deft. his Attorney and says that he cannot deny the writing of the bill of Exchange in the Plaintifs Declaration against him alledged nor but that he owes the said Plaintif the sum of Fifty pounds five shillings and nine pence Sterling like as the said Plaintif in his Declaration aforesaid against him complains Therefore its considered by the Court that the Plaintif recover against the aforesaid Defendant the aforesaid sum of money with Interest thereon after the rate of ten percent per annum from the twenty fifth day of May one thousand seven hundred and sixty two untill this day and five percent from now till paid which he is ordered to pay unto the said Plaintif and also his cost by him in this behalf expended Staying Execution till September next

This Judgment may be discharged in currency at the rate of sixty percent for the difference of exchange

JAMES BOWIE Plaintif against HENRY MILLS & GARRET HACKETT Defendt. On Petition. The Plaintif having proved his demand, Judgment is granted him against the said Defendants in the sum of four pounds sixteen shillings and seven pence half penny current money which they are ordered to pay unto the sd Plaintif with cost

WILLIAM HARRISON Plaintif against JOHN BENGER Defendant On Petition Judgment is granted the Plaintif agst. the Defendant for the sum of three pounds six shillings & three pence which he is ordered to pay with an attorneys fee and cost

Page 175. Caroline County Court 15th day of June 1764

In the Scire Facias sued out by ROGER DIXON gent Coroner a judgment of this County Court granted him against WM. JOHNSTON JUNIOR the twelfth day of March one thousand seven hundred and sixty two for the sum of Seventeen pounds Seventeen shillings and two pence current money fifteen shillings or one hundred and fifty pounds of Tobacco for an attorneys fee and four hundred and thirty nine pounds of Neat tobacco and the Sherif haveing made return on the said Suit that he executed according to Law upon which its considered by the Court that Judgment be renewed and the said Plaintif against the aforesaid Defendant for the above mentioned sum of money and tobacco aforesaid and also his cost by him in this behalf expended and that he may have execution on the same with cost

JAMES DANIEL Defendant against GEORGE MAJOR Defendant On Petition Judgment is granted the Plaintif against the said Defendant for the sum of four pounds ten shillings current money which he is ordered to pay unto the said Plaintif with an attorneys fee and cost

This Judgment except the cost is to be discharged on the Defendants paying the sum of two pounds five shillings current money with Interest thereon from the 2 day of March 1763 till paid

Page 176. Caroline County Court 15th day of June 1764

JAMES DANIEL Plaintif against GEORGE BROOKE Defendant On Petition This suit is dismissed

JOHN POWER and ELENOR his Wife she being first privately examined acknowledged their Deed Indented to ANDREW MUNROSE which on his motion is admitted to record

ARCHIBALD McCALL Plaintif against HENRY EUBANK Defendant On a Petition

This suit is dismissed

JOHN ELLIOT PAINE Plaintif against EDWARD BAKER Defendant On an Attachment. The Defendt. confest Judgment to the said Plaintif for the sum of one pound thirteen shillings and four pence half penny and also his costs by him in this behalf expended

CHARLES WALDEN Plaintif against THOMAS BOOTH & JOHN RICHARDS Defendts. In Debt. And now at this day came the aforesaid Defendants and says that they cannot deny the writing Obligatory in the Plaintifs Declaration against them alledged; nor but that they owe the said Plt. the sum of one hundred and forty two pounds current money like as the said Plaintif in his declaration aforesaid against them complains; therefore its considered by the Court that the Plaintif recover against the aforesd Defendants the aforesaid sum of money and also his

Page 177. Caroline County Court 15th day of June 1764

cost by them in this behalf expended Staying Execution three months

This Judgment except the cost is to be discharged on the Defendants paying the sum of Seventy one pounds current money with lawfull Interest thereon from the fourteenth day of July one thousand seven hundred and sixty three till paid

ROBERT TALIAFERRO Plaintif against SAMUEL NORMANT Defendant. On a Petition. This suit is dismissed

JOHN GRAYHAM Plaintif against RICHARD TANKERSLEY Defendt. In Debt

This day came the aforesaid Defendant and says that he cannot deny the writing Obligatory in the Plaintifs Declaration mentioned nor but he owes the said Plaintif the sum of Eighteen pounds ten shillings and two pence current money like as the said Plaintif in his Declaration aforesaid against him complains therefore its considered by the Court that the Plaintif recover against the said Defendant the aforesaid sum of money and also his cost by him in this behalf expended

This Judgment except the cost is to be discharged on the Defendants paying the sum of five pound five shillings and one penny current money with lawfull Interest thereon from the Seventh day of December 1762 till paid

Page 178. Caroline County Court 15th day of June 1764

JOHN GRAHAM Plaintif against JEREMIAH KENNADAY Deft. In Debt

This day came the aforesaid Defendant and says that he cannot deny the writing Obligatory in the Plaintifs Declaration mentioned nor but he owes the said Plaintif the sum of twenty eight pounds four shillings and two pence current money like as the said Plaintif in his Declaration aforesaid against him complains Therefore its considered by the Court that the Plaintif recover against the aforesaid Defendant the aforesaid sum of money and also his cost by him in this behalf expended Staying Execution three months

This Judgment except the cost is to be discharged on payment of fourteen pounds two shillings and one penny current money with Lawfull Interest thereon from the first day of August one thousand seven hundred and sixty three till paid

ROBERT GILCHRIST gent Plaintif against JAMES GOUCH Defendant. Trespass on the Case. This suit is dismissed being agreed

On the motion of ADAM MERRIMAN an evidence for BENJAMIN ALSOP against CATLETT he haveing attended six days its ordered that the said ALSOP pay him one hundred and fifty pounds of Tobacco for the same

ROGER DIXON Plaintif against JOHN PATROSS Defendant On a Petition

This suit is dismissed

Page 179. Caroline County Court 15th day of June 1764

MATTHEW BOGLE Plaintif against THOMAS SPANIEL Defendant On an Attachment. Judgment is granted the Plaintif against the sd Defendant for the sum of thirteen pounds fifteen shillings and eight pence current money therefore its considered by the Court that the Plaintif recover against the said Defendant the aforesaid sum of money and also his cost by him in this behalf expended

The Sherif haveing made return on the said Attachment that he attached in the hands of WILLIAM POE and the said WILLIAM POE haveing appeared and being sworn as garnishee declares that he has in his hands of the Defendants Estate nine pounds and its ordered that the said garnishee deliver the same to the said Plaintif and he be discharged and make report

JOHN GRAHAM Plaintif against JOHN ROYSTON Defendant On Petition

On the Plaintif proveing his demand, Judgment is granted him against the said Defendant for the sum of two pounds five shillings and nine pence half penny current money and also his cost by him in this behalf expended

Page 180. Caroline County Court 15th day of June 1764

JOHN GRAHAM Plaintif against REUBEN CATLETT Defendant On Petition

The Plaintif haveing proved his demand, Judgment is granted him against the said Defendant for the sum of three pounds three shillings and six pence current money which he is ordered to pay unto the said Plaintif with costs

JOHN GRAHAM Plaintif against JOHN ROYSTON Defendant. In Debt

This day came the aforesaid Defendant and says that he cannot deny the writing Obligatory in the Plaintifs declaration against him alledged nor but that he owes the said Plaintif the full and just sum of fifty nine pounds Eleven shillings current money therefore its considered by the Court that the Plaintif recover against the aforesaid Defendant the aforesaid sum of money and also his cost by him in this behalf expended

This Judgment except the cost is to be discharged on the Defendants paying the sum of twenty nine pounds fifteen shillings and six pence current money with lawfull Interest thereon from the Eighth of November one thousand seven hundred and sixty two till paid

Page 181. Caroline County Court 15th day of June 1764

JAMES MILLER Plaintif against WILLIAM CATLETT Defendant On a Petition

The Plaintif haveing first proved his demand upon which Judgment is granted the Plaintif against the said Defendant for the sum of three pounds fifteen shillings and one penny current money which he is ordered to pay unto the said Plt. with cost

JEFFREY WARRINAH Plaintif against CHESLEY COLEBURN Defendant On a Petition. Judgment is granted the Plaintif against the said Defendant for his cost by him in this behalf expended and an attorneys fee

THOMAS WALLER Plaintif against DARBY SULLIVAN Defendant On a Petition

Judgment is granted the Plaintif against the Defendant for the sum of two pounds seventeen shillings and five pence half penny current money which he is ordered to pay with an attorneys fee and costs

JOHN RICHARDS Plaintif against JOHN ELLIOT PAINE Defendant. On a Petition

This suit is dismissed

Page 182. Caroline County Court 15th day of June 1764

JOHN RICHARDS Plaintif against RALPH FARMER Defendant. On Petition The Plaintif haveing proved his demand Judgment is granted him against the said Defendant for the sum of one pound fourteen shillings and eleven pence half penny current money which he is ordered to pay with an attorneys fee and cost

On the motion of PHILLIP RICHARDS an evidence for JOHN RICHARDS against RALPH FARMER he haveing attended two days and hath come and returned twenty two miles once its ordered that the said RICHARDS pay him one hundred and sixteen pounds of Tobo for the same

JOHN LAWSON Plaintif against JOSEPH DILLARD Defendant In Debt This suit is dismissed

JOHN MULLIN Plaintif against JOSEPH DILLARD Defendant In Debt This suit is dismissed

In the Scire Facias sued out by AMBROSE and CHARLES HUTCHESON to renew a Judgment of this County Court granted them the thirteenth day of August one thousand seven hundred and sixty two against JOHN and WILLIAM WIATT for the sum of one pound twelve shillings and nine pence current money and fifty pounds of Neat Tobo and the Sherif haveing

Page 183. Caroline County Court 15th day of June 1764

made return on the said Writ that he executed according to Law upon which Judgment its considered by the Court that the Plt. recover against the aforesaid Defendant for the aforesaid sum of money and Tobo and also his cost by him in this behalf expended and that he may have exe. for the same

In the Scire Facias sued out by AMBROSE and CHARLES HUTCHESON to renew a Judgment of this County Court granted against JOHN THILMAN and ROBERT MICKLE-BERRY for the sum of Sixteen pounds Eight shillings and six pence current money with Int. from the 20 of June 1762 till paid fifteen shillings or one hundred and fifty pounds of Tobo. for an Attorney fee and one hundred & fififty five pounds of tobacco for costs and the Sherif haveing made return on the said Writ that he executed according to Law upon which its considered by the Court that Judgment be renewed unto the said Plaintif for the aforesaid sum of money and Tobo. and also their cost by them in this behalf expended and they have have Exe. for the same

ROBERT GILCHRIST gent Plaintif against BENJAMIN & WILLIAM WHITEHEAD Defendants On an Attachment. Judgment is granted the Plaintif against the said Defendants for the sum of Six pounds nineteen shillings and ten pence current money and also his cost by him in this behalf expended

And the Sherif haveing made return on the said Writ that he executed it in the hands of RICHARD HEWLETT

Page 184 Caroline County Court 15th day of June 1764

and the said RICHARD HEWLETT by note says he has in his hands of the Defendants Estate four pounds six shillings and six pence current money and its ordered that the said Garnishee deliver the same to the said Plaintif to go in satisfaction of the aforesaid Debt and cost and make report

JOHN BOWCOCK Plaintif against PETER BULLARD Defendant. On Petition Judgment is granted the Plt. against the said Defendant for the sum of two pounds fifteen shillings and ten pence current money which he is ordered to pay unto the said

Plaintif with cost
This Judgment except the cost is to be discharged on the Defts. paying the sum of one pound seven shillings and Eleven pence current money with Interest thereon from the 26 day of March 1763 till paid

(?Furnea) SOUTHALL Plaintif against THOMAS BOOTH Defendant Trespass on the Case And now at this day came the aforesaid Defendant and says he cannot deny the Writing of the account in the Plaintifs declaration against him alledged nor but he owes the said Plaintif the sum of twenty six pounds five shillings current money like as the said Plaintif in his declaration aforesaid against him complians, therefore its considered by the Court that the said Plaintif recover against the said Deft. the aforesaid sum of money and also his cost by him in

Page 185. Caroline County Court 15th June 1764

this behalf expended. Stg. Exe. three months

CUNNINGHAM Plaintif against JAMES MURRAY Defendant Trespass on the Case And now at this day came the aforesaid Defendant and says he cannot deny the Writing in the account in the Plaintifs declaration mentioned nor but that he owes the said Plaintif the sum of Seven pounds Eight shillings and five pence current money like as the said Plaintif in his Declaration aforesaid against him complains therefore its considered by the Court that the Plaintif recover against the said Defendant the aforesaid sum of money and also his cost by him in this behalf expended

TARLTON BROWN Plaintif against GEORGE TRIBBLE Defendant On Petition Judgment is granted the Plaintif against the Defendant for the sum of four pounds twelve shillings current money with Interest thereon from the twenty fourth day of December one thousand seven hundred and sixty three till paid which he is ordered to pay with an Attorney fee and cost

ROBERT GILCHRIST Plaintif against WILLIAM MARTIN & GILES SAMUEL Debt This Suit is agreed

Page 186. Caroline County Court 15th day of June 1764

ROBERT GILCHRIST Plaintif against JACOB LOVEL Defendant On Petition The Defendant appearing in Court confest Judgment to the Plaintif for three pounds two shillings and four pence current money which he is ordered to pay unto the said Plaintif with cost

ROBERT GILCHRIST Plaintif against THOMAS ROYSTON On Petition Judgment is granted the Plaintif against the Defendant for the sum of four pounds seven shillings and eight pence half penny current money which he is ordered to pay with cost

ROBERT GILCHRIST Plaintif against JAMES CARTER On Petition Judgment is granted the Plaintif against the Defendant for two pounds ten shillings and five pence current money which he is ordered to pay with costs

JOHN GRAHAM against WILLIAM BROWN On Petition This suite is dismissed

HENRY RAINS against FRANCIS HUDGINS On Petition This suit is dismissed

Page 187. Caroline County Court 15th day of June 1764

WILLIAM BOWLER against JOHN PICKETT In Trespass

This suit is dismissed being agreed.

ANDREW ANDERSON against CHESLEY COLEBURN Trespass on the Case

This suit is agreed the Defendt. paying cost

CARR McGEEHEE against WILLIAM STEPHENS On Petition

The Plaintif haveing proved his account upon which Judgment is granted him against the Defendt. for two pounds eighteen shillings and four pence current money which he is ordered to pay with costs

JAMES GILBART against JOHN JONES Trespass on the case

This suit is dismissed

JAMES GILBART against WILLIAM PLUNKETT On a Petition

This Suit is dismissed

JAMES GILBART against ROBERT DURRETT Trespass on the Case

This suit is dismissed

Page 188. Caroline County Court 15th day of June 1764

AMBROSE JONES Plaintif against (E?) WHITLOCK & JNO. WOOLFOLK In Debt

The Defendt. confest Judgment to the Plt. for Six pounds seventeen shillings therefore its considered by the Court that the Plaintif recover of the sd Deft. the aforesaid sum of money and also his cost by him in this behalf expended

This Judgment except the cost is to be discharged on paymt. of three pounds eight shillings and six pence current money with Interest from the Tenth day of April 1764 till paid

THOMAS CRANK against LAIRD GORDEN On Petition

Judgment is granted the Plaintif against the Defendant for the sum of one pound sixteen shillings current money with Interest thereon from the thirteenth day of April 1764 till paid which he is ordered to pay unto the said Plaintif with cost

RICHARD (D?) against ABRAHAM MARTIN On Petition

This suit is dismissed

PATRICK HENRY against THOMAS BOOTH On Petition

Judgment is granted the Plaintif for the sum of two pounds current money which he is ordered to pay unto the said Plaintif with an attorney fee and cost

Page 189. Caroline County Court 15th day of June 1764

On the motion of SUSANNAH and JAMES MARTIN evidences for ABRAHAM MARTIN at the suit of (?DORNEN) they haveing attended one day each therefore ordered the said MARTIN pay them fifty pounds of Tobo for the same

THOMAS BOSWELL against THOMAS BOOTH On Petition

The Defendt. confest Judgment to the Plaintif for the sum of three pounds four Shillings & ten pence current money which he is ordered to pay unto the Plaintif with an attorneys fee and cost

WILLIAM BOSWELL against JOHN ELLIOT PAINE In Debt

This day came the aforesaid Defendant and says he cannot deny the writing Obligatory in the Plaintifs declaration mentioned nor but he owes the Plaintif the sum of Seventeen pounds current money therefore its considered by the Court that the Plaintif recover against the said Defendant the aforesaid sum of money

THOMAS PRICE against ROBERT CHEWNING. On Petition

Judgment is granted the Plaintif against the Defendant for the sum of fifteen shillings and sixty nine pounds of Neat Tobo which he is ordered to pay with an attorneys fee and costs

Page 190. Caroline County Court 15th day of June 1764

TERRELLs Executors etc. against RICHARD ROY On a Scire Facias
The Sherif haveing made return on the said Writ that he Executed it according to Law upon which Judgment is granted the Plt. against the Defendant for the sum of seven pounds three shillings and six pence current money with Interest thereon from the first day of October one thousand seven hundred and sixty one till paid also fifteen shillings or one hundred and fifty pounds of Tobo for an attorneys fee and one hundred pounds of Neat Tobo it being the principal Sum of money and tobo cost which the Plaintif recovered a Judgment for against the aforesaid Defendt. the 14th day of May 1762. Therefore its considered by the Court that Judgment be renewed unto the said Plaintif for the aforesd sum of money and Tobo as aforesaid and also his cost by him in this behalf expended and that he may have execution for the same with costs

ANDREW COCKRAN against JOSEPH PRICE On Petition
Judgment is granted the Plaintif against the Deft. for the sum of three pounds four shillings current money which he is ordered to pay with an attorneys fee and costs

JOHN RICHARDS against JOHN GANT Trespass on the Case
The Defendant by a note from under his hand confest Judgment to the Plaintif for the sum of thirty pounds eleven shillings and six pence farthing current money with Interest from the 26 day of May 1764 till paid Staying Execution three months therefore its considered by the Court that the Plaintif recover against the Defendant the aforesaid sum of money and also his cost by him in this behalf expended

Page 191. Caroline County Court 15th day of June 1764

JOHN RICHARDS against WILLIAM COLEBURN. On Petition
The Plaintif haveing proved his demand Judgment is granted him against the Defendant for the sum of two pounds fourteen shillings and two pence current money which he is ordered to pay with an attorneys fee and cost

JOHN RICHARDS against THOMAS STRATTON In Debt
The Defendt. confest Judgment to the Plaintif for the sum of Eight pounds twelve shillings and one pence current money therefore its considered by the Court that the Plaintif recover against the Defendant the aforesaid sum of money and also his cost by him in this behalf expended
This Judgment except the cost is to be discharged on payment of four pounds six shillings and three pence current money with Interest thereon from the first day of December 1762 till paid

JOHN RICHARDS against EUSIBEAS STONE Trespass on the Case
The Defendant by a note from under his hand confest Judgment to the said Plaintif for the sum of Thirty five pounds Six shillings and six pence three farthings current money with lawfull Interest thereon from the Tenth day of May 1764 till paid Staying Exe. four months, therefore its considered by the Court that the Plaintif recover against the Defendant the aforesaid sum of money and also his cost by him in this behalf expended

Page 192. Caroline County Court 15th day of June 1764

JOHN RICHARDS against EDWARD BUCKLEY Trespass on the Case
The Defendant confest Judgment to the Plaintif for the sum of eight pounds thirteen shillings and four pence half penny current money with staying execution three months therefore its considered by the Court that the Plaintif recover against the said

Defendant the aforesaid sum of money and also his cost by him in this behalf expended

JOHN RICHARDS against THADDEUS PRUETT On Petition

The Plaintif haveing proved his demand, Judgment is granted him against the Defendant for the sum of four pounds seven shillings and six pence half penny current money which he is ordered to pay unto the said Plaintif with an attorneys fee and cost

JOHN RICHARDS against JOHN PRUETT SENR. On Petition

The Plaintif haveing proved his demand, Judgment is granted him against the said Defendant for the sum of four pounds five shillings and one penny current money which he is ordered to pay with an attorneys fee and cost

WILLIAM HARRISON against JOHN SCANDLAND On Petition

Judgment is granted the plaintif against the Deft. for the sum of three pounds thirteen shillings and two pence current money which costs he is ordered to pay with costs with Interest thereon from the 15 day of July 1763 till paid

Page 193. Caroline County Court 15th day of June 1764

DAVID PILES Younger against THOMAS AYRES In Debt

The Defendant came into open Court and confest Judgmt. to the Plaintif for the sum of Ten pounds current money therefore its considered by the Court that the Plaintif recover against the said Deft. the aforesaid sum of money and also his cost by him in this behalf expended

This Judgment except the cost is to be discharged on the Defendants paying the sum of five pounds current money with Interest thereon from the first day of July 1763 till paid

JOHN RICHARDS against WILLIAM BROWN Case

This suit is dismissed

JOSEPH WIATT against JOHN WILY On Petition

Judgment is granted the Plaintif against the Defendant for the sum of six pounds ten shillings current money and seventy six pounds of Neat Tobo and Seven Shillings and six pence which is due upon a former Judgment which he is ordered to pay with an attorneys fee and cost

JAMES MILLER against JOHN GRIFFIN On Petition

The Plaintif haveing proved his demand, Judgmt. is granted him against the Defendant for the sum of two pounds one Shilling and one penny current money which he is ordered to pay with cost

Page 194. Caroline County Court 15th day of June 1764

JAMES MILLER against JOSIAH ROGERS On Petition

The Plaintif having proved his demand, Judgment is granted the said Plaintif against the Defendant for the sum of four pounds eight shillings three pence current money which he is ordered to pay unto the said Plaintif with costs

JAMES BALL Assee of THOMAS POWELL against JOHN POWELL On a Scire Facias

The Sherif haveing made return on the said Writ in that he executed it according to Law upon which Judgment is granted the Plaintif against the Defendant for the sum of two pounds eight shillings and eleven pence current money also seven shillings and six pence and seventy seven pounds of Nt. Tobo. which is due upon a former Judgment obtained by the Plaintif against the Defendant the fourteenth day of June 1759 for the sum of money and Tobacco aforesaid therefore its considered by the Court that Judgment be renewed unto the said Plaintif for the aforesd sum of money and Tobo and also his cost by him in this behalf expended and that he may recover the same with costs

ROBERT GILCHRIST against JOHN EVANS Debt
Dismissed being agreed

Page 195. Caroline County Court 15th June 1764

BENJAMIN JOHNSTON against JOSEPH GRESHAM (too faded to read)
This suit is dismissed

JAMES HARRISON against JAMES JOHNSTON On Petition
Judgment is granted the Plaintif against the Defendant for the sum of four pounds sixteen shillings current money which he is ordered to pay with an attorneys fee and cost staying execution three months

ARCHIBALD McCALL against JOHN E. PAINE On Petition
Judgment is granted the Plaintif against the Defendant for the sum of seventy three pounds of Neat Tobo and three pounds Eleven shillings and one half penny current money which he is ordered to pay with an attorneys fee and cost

BENJAMIN HUBBARD against WILLIAM EDRINGTON On a Scire Facias
The Sherif haveing made return on the said Writ that he executed it according to Law upon which its considered that the Judgment of September Court 1760 be renewed unto the said Plaintif for the sum of five pounds eighteen shillings and eight pence current money also fifteen shillings or one hundred and fifty pounds of Tobo for an attorneys fee and one hundred and sixy one pounds of Tobo for costs which he is ordered to pay (remainder of entry too faded)

Page 196. Caroline County Court 15th day of June 1764

(the first entry is too faded to read)

JOHN ELLIOT PAINE against JOHN RICHARDS Trespass on the Case
This suit is dismissed by return of the Writ

JAMES MILLER against RICHARD CLATTERBURK On Petition
The Plaintif haveing proved his demand Judgt. is granted him against the said Defendant for the sum of one pound twelve shillings and three pence current money which he is ordered to pay unto the said Plaintif with costs

BENJAMIN WINSLOW against JOHN WALLER In Debt
By consent of parties and by the Order of Caroline County Court the Suit was referred to OLIVER TOWLES JUNR. to arbitrate and in case of default of either of the parties to proceed upon the part of the partie present who in obedience to the said Order have settled the matter in differance between the parties and finds there is a ballance of fifty four pounds Current money and I do award order & adjudge that the said Defendant pay the aforesaid sum of money together with lawfull interest thereon from the 25th day of December 1761 till paid and the cost of this suit in this behalf expended.
O. TOWLES JR. June the 14th 1764 which award the Court doth confirm

Page 197. Caroline County Court 15th day of June 1764

MARTHA TUTT against WILLIAM TUTT On Petition
This suit is dismissed

JAMES GILBART against DANIEL BARKSDALE Trespass on the case
On the Plaintifs proving his demand, Judgment is granted him against the said Defendant for the sum of seven pounds nineteen shillings and one farthing Sterling which he is ordered to pay unto the said Plaintif and also his cost by him in this behalf expended

This Judgment may be discharged in currency at the rate of 60 percent for the differance of Exchange

ANDREW JOHNSTON Plaintif against JOHN FERGUSON Deft. Case

The Sherif made return on the said Writ that he executed it and the said Defendt. being so warned and now at this day being solemnly called and failing to appear but makeing default its considered by the Court that the Plaintif recover against the Defendt. the sum of Six pounds three shillings and seven pence three farthings current money and also his costs by him in this behalf expended and the said Defendt. in mercy etc.

Ordered that the Court be adjourned untill the Court in Course

RO. GILCHRIST

Page 198. Caroline County Court 7th day of July 1764

At a Court of Oyer and Terminer for Caroline County on Saturday the seventh day of July 1764 upon the Trial of Hannah a Negroe woman Slave belonging to SAMUEL SUTTON of the County of Caroline on Suspicion of feloniously burning the house of the said SAMUEL SUTTON Present

EDMUND PENDLETON ROBERT GILCHRIST)
JAMES JAMESON WILLIAM PARKER &) Gentlemen Justices
JOHN TAYLOR

Hannah a Negroe Woman Slave belonging to SAMUEL SUTTON of the County of Caroline being committed to the Goal of this County by a mittimus from under the hand of WILLIAM TYLER Gent one of his Majesties Justices of the peace for the aforesaid County on Suspicion of her feloniously burning the House of the sd SUTTON and being brought before this Court for trial the said Hannah on her arraignment pleaded not guilty

Whereupon the Court proceeded to examined the witnesses against her: its the opinion of the Court that the said Hannah is Guilty of the facts in the Indictment; therefore its ordered that Sherif cause the said Hannah to be hanged up by the neck until she be dead

The said Hannah is valued to forty pounds current money which is ordered to be certified to the next Assembly

EDMUND PENDLETON

Page 199. Caroline County Court 12th day of July 1764

At a Court held for Caroline County the 12th day of July 1764

Present EDMUND PENDLETON)
ROBERT GILCHRIST) Gent his Majesties Justices
ANTHONY THORNTON &)
JAMES TAYLOR

On the motion of WILLIAM JOHNSTON the several dispositions to the claim of RICHARD GOODE with the Governours Testimonial thereto is ordered to be recorded

JOHN SANDERS JUNR. is appointed overseer of the Road from Mrs. MICOUs old field to the foot of Mrs. TALIAFERROs Hill and its ord'd that he keep the same in repair according to Law

An Indenture of Apprenticeship between RICE POE and JOHN ROY was approved by the Court acknowledged by the parties and ordered to be recorded

ANDREW COCKRAN Plaintif against JAMES GEORGE Defendant Trespass on the Case. Judgment is granted the Plaintif against the Defendant for his cost by him in this behalf expended

Present JOHN TAYLOR Gent

The Inventory and appraisement of the Estate of JOHN HOLLOWAY deceased was this day returned and admitted to record

ANDREW HENDERSON v JOHN CARTER SENR. is dismissed the Deft. paying costs

Page 200. Caroline County Court 12th day of July 1764

RICHARD HEWLETT and JEMIMA his Wife she being first privately examined acknowledged their deed indented to JAMES DISMUKES JUNR. and its ordered to be recorded

THOMAS ROANE Plaintif against THOMAS BOOTH JUNR. and FRAS. FLEMING Defendts. In Debt. And now at this day came the aforesaid Defendants and says that they cannot deny the writing Obligatory in the Plaintifs declaration mentioned, nor but they owe the said Plaintif the sum of two hundred pounds current money like as the said Plaintif in his declaration aforesaid against them complains, therefore its considered by the Court that the Plaintif recover against the Defendants the aforesd sum of money and also his cost by him in this behalf expended

This Judgment except the cost is to be discharged on the said Defendants paying the said Plaintif the sum of fifteen pounds current money with lawful Interest thereon from the 30th day of December 1762 till paid

JOHN CALLAGHAM Plaintif against BETTESWORTH GRASTY Defendt. Trespass on the Case. This day a Jury being impannelled and sworn by name WILLIAM PLUNKETT etc who haveing heard the arguments and evidences of each partie withdrew and in a short time returned the following Verdict (to wit) We the Jury find for the Plt. five pounds current money Damage. WM. PLUNKETT foreman. which Verdict on the Plaintifs motion is admitted to record.

Page 201. Caroline County Court 12th day of July 1764

Therefore its considered by the Court that the Plaintif recover against the said Defendant the aforesaid sum of money by the Jury in their Verdict aforesaid assessed also his cost by him in this behalf expended

ANDREW ANDERSON Plaintif against WILLIAM BOWLER Defendt. Trespass on the Case. The Defendant appeared in open Court and confest Judgment to the said Plaintif for the sum of thirty four pounds ten shillings and five pence farthing current money therefore its considered by the Court that the Plaintif recover against the Defendt. the aforesaid sum of money and also his cost by him in this behalf expended

WILLIAM SPILLER against JOSEPH DEJARANETT In a Petition

On the Plaintifs proveing his demand, Judgment is granted him against the Defendant for the sum of one pound eight shillings and eleven pence half penny current money which he is ordered to pay unto the said Plaintif with an attorneys fee and cost

RICHARD GOODE acknowledged his bond and Power of Attorney to WILLIAM JOHNSTON and its ordered to be recorded

Page 202. Caroline County Court 12th day of July 1764

PAUL THILMAN against GEORGE PEA Trespass on the Case

By consent of the parties and by order of Caroline County Court this suit was referred to EDMUND PENDLETON to arbitrate and settle who haveing returned his Award in these words: I have heard the parties and their evidences and examined their accounts and considered the same and do award that the Defendant pay unto the Plaintif three pounds three shillings and five pence and costs it appearing the Defendant delayed to settle accounts and I do further award that what money shall be collected for the debts now outstanding on the Ordinary Bookes be equally devided between the parties Given under my hand this 15 day of May 1764. EDMUND PENDLETON. which award the Court doth confirm

JAMES BOSWELL against THOMAS BOOTH Trespass on the Case

This day came as well the said Plaintif by his Attorney as the said Defendant by his Attorney and the sd Defendant confessing that he cannot gain say the action of the said Plaintif nor but that the said Plaintif hath sustained damage by reason of not performing of the promise and assumption in the Plaintifs Decln. mentioned to Six pounds nine shillings and two pence current money and the said Plaintif agreeing to take Judgment for that sum, therefore its considered by the Justices here that the said Plaintif recover against the Deft. the aforesaid sum of money and also his cost that he hath sustained in this suit.

Page 203. Caroline County Court 12th day of July 1764

THOMAS ROANE Plaintif against THOMAS BOOTH & FRANCIS FLEMING Defendts. In Debt. And now this day came the parties by their attorneys and mutually agreed to wave the Issue to the Countrey and submit the matter to the Judgment of the Court Whereupon all and singular the premises being seen and by the Court fully understood and mature deliberation being thereunto had its considered that the said THOMAS ROANE recover against the said THOMAS BOOTH and FRANCIS FLEMING the sum of three hundred pounds current money and also his cost by him in this behalf expended

This Judgment except the cost is to be discharged on the Defendants THOMAS BOOTH and FRANCIS FLEMING paying the sum of Sixteen pounds Seventeen shillings with Interest thereon from the 30th day of December 1762 till paid

THOMAS WHITING Plaintif against LUDWELL GRIMES Defendt. In Debt (This entry is very faded. The original entry has been lined through and some writing appears in the margin apparently to replace what had been originally written.)

Page 204. Caroline County Court 12th day of July 1764

(the previous entry is continued with more deletions and new figures inserted) sum of two hundred and forty three pounds five shillings Sterling it being the Ballance of the Protest of the Bill of Exchange in the Plaintifs Declaration mentioned with Lawfull Interest thereon after the rate of five percent per annum from the 12th day of July one thousand seven hundred and sixty four untill paid and also his cost by him in this behalf expended

This Judgment may be discharged in Currency at the rate of Sixty percent for the Difference of Exchange

The Inventory and appraisement of the Estate of DANIEL TOMPKINS deceased was this day returned and admitted to record

On the motion of ELIZABETH SMITHER an evidence for JOHN CALLAHAN against BETTESWORTH GRASTY she haveing attended nine days and hath come and returned fifteen miles nine times its therefore ord'd that the said JOHN CALLAGHAM pay her six hundred and thirty pounds of Tobo for the same

JOHN BAIRD Plaintif against WILLIAM JOHNSON, BENJAMIN JOHNSON and FRANCIS COLEMAN In Case. This Suit by Order of Caroline County Court and by consent of the parties was referred for Determination of EDMUND PENDLETON Gent to audit state and settle the same and his award was to

Page 205. Caroline County Court 12th day of July 1764

be returned and was to be made the Judgment of the Court and the Auditor his award returned in the following words This suit was referred to my determination I have heard the parties and the witnesses and examined the ( ) and settled the same and award that the Plaintif recover against the said Defendants forty Seven pounds five Shillings and three pence current money and costs of this suit. Given under my hand this 12 day of July 1764 EDMUND PENDLETON, which award the Court doth confirm

JOHN BAIRD Plaintif against WM. JOHNSTON, BENJA. JOHNSTON & FRAS. COLEMAN Defts. In Debt. This Suit by consent of the parties and by the Order of the Caroline County Court was referred to the determination of EDMUND PENDLETON Gent to arbitrate and settle who haveing returned his Award in the following manner This suit was referred to me to arbitrate and settle I heard the parties and their evidences and duly considered the same and do award that the Plaintif recover against the Defendants four hundred and Sixteen pounds Eleven shillings and cost of this suit which he will sustain. This Judgment except the costs to be discharged on payment of ninety four pounds one shilling five pence with Interest thereon from the 2d of ( ) 1760 which award the Court doth confirm (the material on this page is very faded)

Page 206. Caroline County Court 12th day of July 1764

On the complaint of WILLIAM BARBER against JOHN WILY to continue to next Court and its ordered that the said WILY suffer him to appear at the next Court to ( ) for the sd County and that he not abuse him

CONWAYS Exors. Plaintif against THOMAS SCOTT Defendant. In Case This day came as well the Plaintif by his Attorney as the said Defendant by his Attorney and the said Defendant confessing that he cannot gainsay the action aforesaid of the said Plaintif nor but the said Plaintif hath sustained damage by reason of his not performing and assumption in the declaration mentioned ten pounds current money and the said Plaintif agreeing to take judgment for that sum therefore its considered by the Justices here that the said Plaintif recover against the said Defendant the aforesaid sum of Ten pounds Current money aforesaid and further its considered by the Justices here that the said Plaintif recover against the said Defendt. his cost by him in this behalf expended and the said Defendant in mercy etc.

JAMES MILLER Assee of COLLIN REDDOCK Plaintif against JAMES TALIAFERRO Defendt. In Debt. This day came the parties by their Attorneys & the said Defendt. waved the issue joined in this suit & confest Judgment to the Plt. for twenty (blacked out)

Page 207. Caroline County Court 12th day of July 1764

pounds current money which he is ordered to pay and his cost by him in this behalf expended and on the motion of the Deft. an Injunction is granted him provided he file his Bill and give Secy

COLLIN REDDOCK Plaintif against ANN & JAMES TALIAFERRO Defents. In Debt And now at this day came as well the said Plaintif by his as the said Defendants by their attorney who mututally agreed to wave the issue to the Country and submit the matter to the Judgment of the Court Whereupon all and singular the premises being seen and by the Court understood and mature deliberation being thereupon had its considered that the said Plaintif recover against the said Defendant the sum of Eleven pounds Seven Shillings and ten pence current money and its further considered that the

Plaintif recover against the Defendant cost by him in his behalf expended
This Judgment except the cost is to be discharged on the payment of Five pounds Thirteen shillings and Eleven pence current money with Interest thereon from the 6th day of Febry. 1759 till paid and on the motion of the Deft and Injunction is granted him to stay the proceedings at common issue provided he file his Bill and give Security by the next Court

ELIZABETH MARRIOTT HUMPHREY Plt. against JOHN MOTHLEY Defendt. In Debt
This day came the parties by their Attorneys & the said

Page 208. Caroline County Court 12th day of July 1764

Defendant waved the issue Joined in this Suit and confest Judgment to the said Plaintif for Seventy four pounds Six shillings and Eight pence Therefore its considered by the Court that the Plaintif recover against the said Defendant the aforesaid Sum of money and also his cost by him in this behalf expended
This Judgment except the cost is to be discharged on payment of Thirty seven pounds Three shillings and Four pence with Interest thereon from the Tenth day of Febry. 1763 till paid

JOHN CHAPMAN Plaintif against THOMAS BOOTH JUNIOR Defendt. In Debt
And now at this day came the parties by their Attorneys and mutually agreed to wave the issue Joind in this suit and submit the matter to the Judgment of the Court and thereupon all and singular the premises being seen and by the Court now here fully understood its considered that the said JOHN recover against the said THOMAS Forty seven pounds current money and also his costs by him in this behalf expended and the said THOMAS in mercy
This Judgment except the cost is to be discharged on the Defendants paying the said Plaintif the sum of Twenty three pounds Ten shillings current money with Lawfull Interest thereon from the first day of March 1763 till paid

Page 209. Caroline County Court 12th day of July 1764

JOHN PRICE Plaintif against JOHN WILY Defendant In Debt
And now at this day came the parties by their Attorneys and mutually agreed to wave the issue by the Country and submit the matter to the Judgt. of the Court whereupon all and singular the premises being seen and by the Court was here fuly understood the declaration being thereunto had its considered that the said JOHN PRICE recover against the said JOHN WILY the sum of Fifty eighty pounds and also his cost by him in this behalf expended and the said Defendant in mercy
This Judgment except the cost is to be discharged on the Defendants paying unto the Plaintif the sum of Twenty nine pounds Current money with Lawfull Interest thereon from the fifteenth day of July one thousand seven hundred and sixty two till paid

JAMES GILBART Plaintiff against THOMAS WATKINS Defendant Trespass on the Case. This day came the parties by their Attorneys and mutually agreed to wave the Issue to the Country and submit the matter to the Judgment of the Court Whereupon all and singular the premises being seen and by the Court now here fuly understood it is considered by the Court that the Plaintif recover against the said Deft. the sum of Forty nine pounds Sixteen shillings and Eleven pence Three farthings Sterling also his cost by him

Page 210. Caroline County Court 12th day of July 1764

in this behalf expended. Exchange at 60 per cent

ANDREW CRAWFORD Assee of JOHN TAYLOR against JOHN SUTTON On Motion Judgment is granted the Plaintif against the Defendant for the sum of Eighty five pounds current money with lawfull Interest thereon from the twelfth day of August 1762 till paid, also Fifteen shillings or one hundred and Fifty pounds of Tobacco for an Attorneys fee and one hundred and Sixty eight pounds of Neat Tobacco for costs which is according to a Judgment obtained by the Plaintif GEORGE WILY (July 1763) Therefore it is considered by the Court that the Plaintif the aforesaid sum of money and also his cost by him in this behalf expended and the said Defendt. in mercy etc. Staying execution four months

This Court be adjourned till tomorrow moring 9 O'clock

EDMUND PENDLETON

Page 211. Caroline County Court 13th day of July 1764

At a Court Continued and held for Caroline County on Friday the 13 day of July 1764 Present EDMUND PENDLETON, JAMES TAYLOR)
JOHN BAYNHAM, GABL. THROCKMORTON) Gent Justices
and JOHN TAYLOR

RICHARD LEKENS (?) Plaintif against JONATHAN DOUGLASS Defendt. In Debt This day clame the parties by their Attorneys and mutually agreed to wave the Issue to the County and submit the matter to the Judgment of the Court whereupon all and singular the premises being seen and by the Court was here fully understood and mature deliberation being had its considered that the Plaintif recover against the Deft. the sum of Seven pounds Eleven Shillings and Six pence half penny current money and also his cost by him in this behalf expended and the said Deft. in mercy

The Inventory and appraisement of the Estate of JOHN MARTIN deceased was this day returned and admitted to record

WILLIAM RICHISON Plt against WILLIAM BOWLER In Case This day came the said Plaintif by his Attorney and the said Defendant by his Attorney and the said Defendant confessing that he cannot

Page 212. Caroline County Court 13th day of July 1764

gain say the action aforesaid of the said Plaintif nor but that the said Plaintif hath sustained damage by reason of his not performing of the premise and assumption in the declaration mentioned to Five pounds Six shillings and Ten pence current money and the said Plaintif agreeing to the Judgment for that Sum therefore its considered by the Justices here that the Plaintif recover against the Defendant the aforesaid sum of Five pounds Six shillings and Ten pence current money and its further considered by the said Justices that the Plt. recover of the said Defendant his cost by him in this behalf expended and the said Defendant in mercy

ANN JONES Plaintif against JOHN TOWNSEND & NATHANIEL NORMENT Defendt. In Debt. This day came the parties by their attorneys and mutually agreed to wave the Issue to the Countrey and submit the matter to the Judgment of the Court whereupon all and singular the premises being seen and by the Court now here fully understood and mature of deliberation being thereupon had its considered that the Plaintif recover against the said Defendants the sum of Fourteen pounds Seven shillings and Six pence and also her cost by her in this behalf expended and the said Defendants in mercy

This Judgment except the cost is to be discharged on the said Defendants paying unto the said Plaintif the sum of Seven pounds Six shillings and Three pence current money with Interest thereon from the 1st day of Apl. 1763 till paid

Page 213. Caroline County Court 13th day of July 1764

STEPHEN LOWE Plaintif against JAMES GEORGE Defendant Debt
This suit is dismissed

WILLIAM CUNNINGHAM Plt against JOHN VICE Defendant In Case
Judgment is granted the Plaintif against the Defendant for the cost in this behalf expended

DUNCAN GRAHAM Plaintif against JOHN WATKINS Defendant In Case
This day came the said Plaintif by his Attorney and a Jury to wit JAMES LINDSEY foreman whereupon the damages sustainded by the Plaintif by reason of the Defendant his not performing the (faded) in the declaration mentioned (faded) and sworn upon their oath do say that the Plaintif hath sustained Damages by reason thereof to Twelve pounds Four shilling and Six pence therefore its considered by the Justices that the said Plaintif recover against the said Defendant and THOMAS WATKINS his Security the sum of Twelve pounds Four shillings Six pence damage afaoresaid in form aforesaid and further by the Justices here its considered that the said Plaintif recover against the said Security THOMAS WATKINS his costs by him in this behalf expended and that the said Deft. and Secty. in mercy

Page 214. Caroline County Court 13th day of July 1764

THOMAS NORMENT being this day admitted to chuse a Guardian made choice of JAMES (inserted above the entry and faded) NORMANT who was approved of by the Court and acknowledged a Bond for the same

A Deed from WILLIAM DUDLEY and PRUDENCE his Wife to JOHN WILY was proved by the oaths of three of the witnesses and ordered to be recorded

A Deed of Sale from BETTESWORTH GRASTY to BENJAMIN HUBBARD was proved by the oaths of the witnesses and ordered to be recorded

WILLIAM BOWLER acknowledged his deed Indented to JOHN BAYLER Esqr. and its admitted to record

JOHN LINDSEY Plaintif against HARRY BEVERLEY Defendt. In Case
And now at this day came as well the said Plaintif by his Attorney as the said Defendant by his Attorney and the Jurrors of a Jury to wit ABRAHAM HARPER foreman who to say the truth upon the premises being elected tried and sworn do say that the said Defendant did assume in upon himself in manner and form as the said Plaintif against him hath complainted and we do assess the Damages of the Plaintifs by reason of the not performing of the promise and assumption aforesaid One hundred and fourteen pounds Three shillings and Eleven pence current money therefore its considered by the Justices here that the said

Page 215. Caroline County Court 13 day of July 1764

Plaintif recover against the said Defendant the aforesaid sum of One hundred and fourteen pounds Three shillings and Eleven pence damages by the Jurors aforesaid in form aforesaid assessed and further by the Justices it is here considered that the Plt. recover against the sd Defendant his cost by him in this behalf expended and the said Defendant in mercy

Our Sovereign Lord the King Plaintif against MARY ANN WEBSTER & NANCY WEBSTER Defts. This day came ZACHARIAH (L) Deputy attorney for our Sovereign Lord as the said Defendants by their Attorney and also the Jurrors of a Jury to wit ROBERT GARROTT foreman who to say the truth of the premises being elected tried and Sworn upon their oaths do say that the said Defendants are not guilty of the assault and Battery in the Indictment set forth Therefore its considered by the Justices here that the said Plaintif take nothing by his Bill aforesaid but for his false clamour be in mercy and that the said Defendt. go thereof without day and further by the Justices its here considered that the said Defendants recover against the said Plaintif his cost by him about this defence in this behalf expended

On the motion of JOHN GRAY an evidence for JOHN LINDSEY against HARRY BEVERLEY he haveing attended nine days and hath come and returned 26 miles four times and four ferriages at Port Royal, its therefore ordered that the said LINDSEY

Page 216. Caroline County Court 13th day of July 1764

pay him five hundred and sixty pounds of Tobo for the same besides the ferriages

On the motion of WILLIAM MULLIN an evidence for HARRY BEVERLEY at the suit of JOHN LINDSEY he haveing attended one day its ordered that the said BEVERLEY pay him twenty five pounds for the same

WILLIAM JOHNSTON Plaintif against JOHN BUCKNER Defendant On Petition The Plaintif by a note from under his hand confest Judgment unto the Plaintif for the sum of Four pounds One Shilling and Six pence half penny current money Therefore its considered by the Justices here that the Plaintif recover against the said Defendant the aforesaid sum of money Interest thereon from the 18th of August 1762 till paid

The Last Will and Testament of CALEB LINDSAY deceased was presented in Court by JAMES ( ) and JOHN MILLER Executors therein named who made oath according to Law and was proved by the Oaths of JOHN BOUTWELL and ELIZABETH BULLING and was ordered to be recorded and the said Exors. performing what is usual in such cases certificate is granted them for obtaining a probate thereof in due form of Law

ISAAC DYER Plaintif against THOMAS LANDRUM Defendt. In Case This day came as well the said

Page 217. Caroline County Court 13th day of July 1764

Plaintif by his Attorney as the said Defendant by his Attorney and the Jurrors of a Jury to wit ABRAHAM HARPER foreman who to say the truth of the premises being elected tryed and Sworn upon their oaths do say that the said Plaintif hath sustained damages by reason of the not performing of the promise and assumption in the Declaration mentioned to Twelve pounds Four shillings and Two pence current money besides his cost therefore its considered by the Justices here that the Plaintif recover against the said Defendant the aforesaid Sum of money by the Jurors in form aforesd assessed and its further considered by the Justices here that the Plaintif recover against the Defendant his cost by him in this behalf expended and the said Defendant in mercy

A Deed from RICHARD DURRETT Indented to JOHN DURRETT was proved by the oaths of three of the witnesses thereto and was ordered to be recorded

A Deed from JOHN DURRETT Indented to RICHARD DURRETT was proved by the oaths of three of the witnesses thereto and ord'd to be recorded

BENJAMIN HUBBARD gent Plaintif against JOHN BOWCOCK Defendant In Debt This day came as well the said Defendant by his Attorney and the said Defendt. confessing that he cannot gain say the action aforesaid of the said Plaintif nor but that the said Plaintif hath sustained damage by

Page 218. Caroline County Court 13th day of July 1764

reason of the not performing of the Debt in the Declaration mentioned to One hundred and Thirty four pounds besides his costs and the Plaintif agreeing to take Judgment for that sum its therefore considered by the Justices that the Plaintif recover the aforesaid sum of money of the said Defendant and cost by him in this behalf expended and the said Defendant in mercy

This Judgment except the cost is to be discharged on the Defendants paying the sum of Sixty six pounds current money with lawfull Interest thereon from the twenty first day of August 1761 until payment

On the motion of DILLARD HARRIS an Evidence for ISAAC DYER against THOMAS LANDRUM he haveing attended two days and hath come and returned twenty miles twice its therefore ordered that the said DYER pay him One hundred and seventy pounds of Tobacco for the same

GEORGE ABRISON Plaintif against JOHN MILLER Defendant In Debt

This day came the parties by their Attorneys and mutually agreed to wave the issue by the Countrey and submit the matter to the Judgment of the Court whereupon all and singular the premises being seen and by the Court fully understood its considered that the Plaintif recover against the said Defendant the sum of Seven pounds Seven shillings current money and also his cost by him in this behalf expended

Page 219. Caroline County Court 13th day of July 1764

On the motion of WILLIAM WRIGHT an Evidence for ISAAC DYER against THOMAS LANDRUM he haveing attended three days its ordered that the said DYER pay him Seventy five pounds of Tobo for the same

ROBERT ROBERTS Plaintif against GABRIEL TOOMBS Defendant In Case

This day came the parties by their Attorneys who mutually agreed to wave the issue to the Country and submit the matter to the Judgment of the Court whereupon all and singular the premises being seen and by the Court fully understood mature of deliberation being thereupon had its considered that the Plaintif recover against the Defendant the sum of Five pounds four Shillings and seven pence current money and also his cost by him in this behalf expended and the said Defendant in mercy

On the motion of JOHN WILY an Injunction is granted him to stay the money in the Sherifs hands due on TRAYNHAMs Exrs. against him upon his filing a Bill of Injunction within three weeks in the Clerks office

JOHN ELLIOT PAINE Plaintif against DAVIS DAVENPORT Defendant On Attachment Judgment is granted the Plaintif against the Defendant for the sum of four pounds two shillings and nine pence half penny current money and also his cost by him in this behalf expended

And the Sherif having made return on the sd

Page 220 Caroline County Court 13th July 1764

Writ that he rendered it in the hands of JOHN PULLAR and summoned him to appear as Garnishee and the said Garnishee appeared and being sworn declares he has in his hands of the Defendants Estate Three pounds Two shillings and four pence half penny current money therefore its ordered that the said Garnishee deliver the same to the said Plaintif and satisfy his Judgment therewith and make report

Ordered the Court be adjourned till the Court in Course
EDMUND PENDLETON

At a Court held for Caroline County on Thursday the 9 day of August 1764
Present EDMUND PENDLETON JAMES TAYLOR)
JAMES JAMESON ROBERT TALIAFERRO) Gentlemen Justices
GABRIEL THROCKMORTON)

The Last Will and Testament of JOHN LUCAS deceased was produced in Court by AMBROSE HUTCHESON Exer. therein named who made oath thereto according to Law and being proved by the oaths of witnesses was admitted to record and the said Exer. performing what is usual in such cases certificate is granted him for obtaining a probate thereof in due form of Law and the sd Exer. acknowledged Bond for the same

Its ordered that WILLIAM CHILES, WALTER CHILES, RICHARD GEORGE & WILLIAM WIATT or any three of them being first duly sworn accordg. to law appraise the Estate of JOHN LUCAS deceased and make report

Page 221. Caroline County Court 9th day of August 1764

Its ordered that JOHN BOUTWELL, RICHARD AHART (?), SIMON MILLER and ROBERT GARROTT or any three of them appraise the estate of CALEB LINDSEY deceased and make report of their proceedings to Court

JOHN LAWSON acknowledged his Deed Indented to THOMAS WORTHAM and admitted to record

JAMES JENNINGS FOSTER and ELIZABETH his Wife she being first privately examined acknowledged their Deed Indented to ISMEL ISBELL and is admitted to record

JAMES MURRY and FRANCES his Wife she being first privately Examined acknowledged their Deed Indented to MATTHEW PEATROSS and is admitted to record

RICHARD WEST returned an account on Oath of the Guardianship of JAMES CRUTCHFIELD Orphan which is admitted to record

PETER MASON returned an account on Oath of the Guardianship of the Orphans of WILLIAM MASON deceased which is ordered to be recorded

WILLIAM TOMPKINS acknowledged his Deed and Receipt endorsed thereon Indented to WILLIAM ELLIS and its admitted to record

NORMAN (   ) returned an account on oath of the Guardianship of JOHN WHITLOCKS Orphans and its admitted to record

ANDESON LIPSCOMB returned an account on oath of Guardianship of THOMAS GEORGE and MARTIN CRUTCHFIELD Orphans which is admitted to record

JOHN MITCHELL acknowledged his Deed and Receipt endorsed thereon Indented to AQUILLA JOHNSTON and its admitted to record

Page 222. Caroline County Court 9th day of August 1764

An Account of the Administration of the estate of JOSEPH and AGNES CROSEs returned by NICHOLAS STONE was examined and approved of by Court and admitted to record

The Inventory and appraisment of the Estate of WILLIAM CRUTCHER deceased was this day returned and admitted to record

JONATHAN SMITH of Drisdale Parish is exempted from paying County levies

JOHN TILLAR of St. Margaretts Parish is exempted from paying County levies

A Bill of Sale from WILLIAM BOSELER to THOMAS POLLARD was proved by the Oath of EDMUND PENDLETON gent and admitted to record

ELLIS GRAVELL returned an account on Oath of the Guardianship of ROSA GRANT Orphan and its admitted to record

On the motion of EDMUND PENDLETON its ordered that BENJAMIN HUBBARD, EUSIBEOUS STONE and JOHN SUTTON settle the account of JOHN and GEORGE HOOMES Orphans and likewise the account of the Administration of the estate of JAMES TAYLOR deceased and make report

The several Inspectors are to continue as recommended last year, the several Sherifs are to continue as recommended last year.

Its Ordered that JAMES TAYLOR Gent Treasurer pay JOHN WILY Eighty four pounds Seventeen shillings and Six pence and also pay BENJAMIN TOMPKINS Twenty pounds in part of his demand in building ( ) bridges and the ballce. of L 29 he is to wait till July 1765 and to receive Int. on the money

Page 223. Caroline County Court 9th day of August 1764

THOMAS SHIP returned an account on Oath of the Guardianship of THOMAS SHIP Orphan of JOSEPH SHIP and its admitted to record

On the motion of AMBROSE JETER an evidence for HARRY BEVERLEY at the Suit of WILLIAM WHITE he haveing attended twelve days its ordered the said BEVERLEY pay him three hundred pounds of Tobacco for the same

On the motion of JOSEPH TANKERSLEY an Evidence for HARRY BEVERLEY at the suit of WILLIAM WHITE he haveing attended thirteen days its ordered that the said BEVERLEY pay him three hundred and twenty five pounds of Tobo. for the same

WILLIAM JOHNSTON Plaintif against THOMAS BURK Defendant On Petition
The Defendant by a note from under his hand confest Judgment to the said Plaintif for the sum of One pounds one shilling three pence half penny current money which he is ordered to pay unto the said Plaintif with costs

On the motion of PETER MASON its ordered that BENJAMIN FAULKNER, MELCH. BRANN and DANIEL ISBELL devide the estate of the Orphans of WILLIAM MASON deceased and make report

FRANCIS HORN Plaintif against EDWARD IRVEN and JAMES BOWIE Deft. In Debt This suit is dismissed

Page 224. Caroline County Court 9th day of August 1764

ANDREW ANDERSON Plaintif against RICHARD BEASLEY Defendant Trespass on the Case. The Defendant appeared in open Court and confest Judgment unto the said Plaintif for the sum of Three pounds Nineteen shillings and Nine pence farthing Currt. money, therefore its ordered by the Court that the Plaintif recover against the said Defendant the aforesaid sum of money and also his cost by him in this behalf expended

JAMES MILLER against JOHN LAWSON Defendant On Petition
The Defendant appeared in open Court and confest Judgment unto the said Plaintif for the sum of Four pounds One shilling and two pence Current monety and the Plaintif being willing to take a Judgment for that sum, its considered by this Court that the Plaintif recover against the Deft. the aforesaid sum of money and also his cost by him in this behalf expended, and the said Defendant in mercy

GEORGE BULLARD Plaintif against THOMAS BURK Defendant Trespass of an Assault & Battery. This suit is dismissed it being agreed

Page 225. Caroline County Court 9th day of August 1764

WILLIAM LIPSCOMB Plaintif against GEORGE WILY Defendant On Petition The Plaintif haveing proved his demand, Judgment is granted him against the Defendant for the sum of One pound Nine shillings and Six pence current money which he is ordered to pay with an Attorneys fee and costs

Its ordered that the Court be adjourned till tomorrow morning nine o clcok

EDMUND PENDLETON

At a Court continued and held for Caroline County Ffriday the Tenth day of August 1764

Present	EDMUND PENDLETON,	JOHN TAYLOR	)
	JOHN BAYNHAM	WILLIAM PARKER	) Gent his Majesties
	GABRIEL THROCKMORTON		) Justices

On the motion of BENJAMIN HUBBARD by JOHN SEMPLE his Attorney against JOHN PICKETT for an injunction in Chancery to stay the proceedings at Common Law on a Judgment obtained by the said PICKETT against the said HUBBARD which injunction the Court granted him upon his giving Bond and security in the Clerks Office

Page 226. Caroline County Court 10th day of August 1764

EDWARD WADE and RACHELL his Wife Complainants against
GEORGE GIBSON & JEREMIAH PEARCE Respondt. Chancery
This Suit is dismissed it being agreed

JAMES GILBART Esqr. Plaintif against WILLIAM HIGGINS Defendant Trespass on the Case. This suit is dismissed

JAMES TERRELL and MARGARETT his Wife Complts. against
JOHN ALMAND Exor. of WATKINS deced Respondt. In Chancery
By consent of the parties and by order of Caroline County Court this suit was refered to the determination of JOHN TAYLOR and JOHN BAYNHAM who was to arbitrate, state and settle the same, and now at this day the auditors returned their award in the following words (to wit) Pursuant we have examined into the personal Estate whereof JOHN WATKINS died possessed of as also the produce since his death while in the Custody of MARY WATKINS and are of opinion that the calculation below will do Justice to JAMES TERRELL or others who claim from the said JOHN WATKINS deceased Estate according to his Will

14 head of Cattle	appraised to	L 14..12..0
34 head hoggs	appraised to	5..13..6
21 head sheep	appraised to	4..18..0
		L 25..3..6
one fourth part of which is deducted		6..5..10 1/2

Page 227. Caroline County Court 10th day of August 1764

We also find personal estate of the value of Eleven pounds five shillings and nine pence which being before devided; that devision JAMES TERRELL agreed to stand to; so that we award to the said TERRELL in consideration of stock only Six pounds Five shillings and ten pence half penny current money as is hereinbefore mentioned. Certified under our hands this 7th day of May 1764. JOHN TAYLOR, JOHN BAYNHAM and its ordered and decreed that the Defendant pay unto the said Plaintif the aforesaid sum of money in manner and form as is in the award mentioned and also his cost by him in this behalf expended and the said Defendant in mercy

DANIEL DEFOE Complainant against ELIZABETH HOLLOWAY Respondt. In Chancery. By consent of the parties its ordered and decreed that JAMES TAYLOR, WILLIAM BUCKNER and WILLIAM WOODFORD or any two of them lay of One hundred acres of land in a reasonable manner so as to include the plantation whereon the said DANIEL now liveth and make report

DAVID CHIVIS Plantif against BENJAMIN ROBINSON Deft. In Debt This day came the parties and agreed to wave the issue by the Countrey and refer the same to the Court and thereupon all and singular the premises being seen and by the Court now here fully understood and mature deliberation being thereupon had its considered that the said DAVID recover against the said

Page 228. Caroline County Court 10th day of August 1764

BENJAMIN Twenty five pounds Seven shillings and eleven pence three farthings current money and also his costs by him in this behalf expended and the said Defendant in mercy

JAMES RENNOLDS Plaintif against JAME GOUGE Defendant In Debt This day came the parties by their Attorneys and mutually agreed to wave the issue to the Countrey and submit the matter to the Judgment of the Court whereupon all and singular the premises being seen and by the Court here fully understood and mature deliberation thereupon had, its considered that the said RENNOLDS recover against the said GOUGE Twenty pounds current money and also his cost by him in this behalf expended and the said Defendant in mercy

This Judgment except the cost is to be discharged on payment of Ten pounds current money with Interest thereon after the rate of five percent per annum from the third day of October 1761 till paid.

On the motion of SAMUEL NORMENT an Evidence for MOSA HURT at the Suit of CARNAL he having attended two days its ordered that the said HURT pay him Fifty pounds of Tobacco for the same

WILLIAM WHITE Plaintif against HARRY BEVERLEY Esqr. Deft. Case This suit is dismissed it being agreed

JOHN BOHANNON Plt. against JEREMIAH PEARCE Deft. Case This suit is dismissed for want of security

Page 229. Caroline County Court 10th day of August 1764

JOHN TAYLOR Merchant Plaintif against JOHN ALEXANDER STILL Defendt. Trespass on the Case. This day came as well the said Plaintif by his Attorney as the said Defendant by his Attorney and the said Defendant confessing that he cannot gainsay the action aforesaid of the said Plaintifs not but that the said Plaintif hath sustained damage by reason of the non performance of the premise and assumption in the Declaration mentioned to Twenty seven pound Nine shillings and Nine pence half penny current money and the said Plaintif agreeing to take Judgment for that sum therefore its considered by the Justices here that the said Plaintif recover against the Defendant the aforesaid sum of Twenty seven pounds Nine shillings and Nine pence half penny damage aforesaid and further it is considered by the Justices here that the said Plaintif recover against the said Defendant his cost by him in this behalf expended and the said Defendant in mercy

Page 230. Caroline County Court 10th day of August 1764

This Judgment except the cost is to be discharged on payment of Twenty two pounds Ten shillings current money with lawfull Interest thereon to be computed after the rate of five percent per annum from the 14th day of April one thousand seven hundred and sixty three untill the same is fully paid

JAMES GILBART Esquier Plaintif against JOHN WILY Trespass on the Case

This day came as well the said Plaintif by his Attorney as the said Defendant by his Attorney and the said Defendant confessing that he cannot gainsay the action aforesaid of the sd Plaintif not but that the said Plaintif hath sustained damage by reason of his non performance of the premises and assumption in the declaration mentioned to Fifty eight pounds Twelve shillings and Six pence half penny Sterling and the said Plaintif agreeing to take Judgment for the sum therefore its considered by the Justices here that the Plt. recover against the Defendant the aforesaid sum of Fifty eight pounds Twelve shillings and Six pence half penny Sterling damage aforesd and further its considered by the Justices here that the Plaintif recover against the said Defendant his cost by him in this behalf expended and the said Defendt. in mercy

This Judgment may be discharged in currency at the rate of Sixty percent for the diference of exchange.

Page 231. Caroline County Order Book 10th day of August 1764

PATRICK COUTTS Plaintif against CHARLES YARBROUGH Defendt. In Debt

This day came the parties by their Attorneys who mutually agreed to wave the Issue by the Countrey and submit the matter to the Judgment of the Court whereupon all and singular the premises being seen and by the Court now here fully understood mature of deliberation thereupon had its considered that the Plaintif recover against the Defendant the sum of Fifteen pounds Thirteen shillings and four pence with Interest on Thirteen pounds part thereof from the eighteenth day of June one thousand seven hundred and sixty three till paid and also his cost by him in this behalf expended and the said Defendant in mercy

PATRICK COUTTS Plaintif against CHARLES YARBROUGH Defendt. In Debt

This day came the parties by their Attorneys who mutually agreed to wave the issue by the Countrey and submitt the matter to the Judgment of the Court whereupon all and singular the premises being seen and by the Court here fully understood mature of deliberation being thereupon had its considered that the Plaintif recover against the said CHARLES Fifty six pounds current money and also his cost by him in this behalf expended and the Defendant in mercy

This Judgment except the cost is to be discharged on payment of Twenty eight pounds Current money with Interest thereon to be computed after the rate of five percent per annum from the first day of April 1763 till payment

Page 232. Caroline County Court 10th day of August 1764

(the first entry on this page is very faded and partially torn away. .... assee of MOSA HURT Plt. against THOMAS JONES and NATHANIEL RITCHISON Deft.)

ANDREW COCKRAN Plaintif against SAMUEL NORMENT Defendant in debt.

This day came the parties by their Attorneys who mutually agreed to wave the Issue to the Countrey and submit the matter to the Judgment of the Court whereupon all and singular the premises being seen and by the Court here fully understood mature delibertion thereupon had its considered that the said ANDREW recover against the said

SAMUEL Fifty seven pounds Thirteen shillings and Eight pence half penny also his cost by him in this behalf expended and the said Defendt. in mercy.

Page 233. Caroline County Court 10th day of August 1764

This Judgment except the cost is to be discharged on payment of Twenty eight pounds Sixteen shillings and Ten pence farthing with Interest to be computed after the rate of five percent per annum from the first day of February one thousand seven hundred and sixty three untill the same is paid

PATRICK CAFFREY Plaintif against JAMES GEORGE Defendt. In Trespass

This day came as well the Plaintif by his Attorney as the said Defendant by his Attorney and the said Deft. confessing that he cannot gainsay the action aforesaid of the said Plt. not but that the said Plaintif hath sustained damage by reason of the trespass in the Declaration mentioned to Twenty Shillings besides his cost and the said Plaintif agreeing to take a Judgment for that sum its considered by the Justices that the Plaintif recover against the said Defendant the aforesaid sum of Twenty shillings damage and also his cost by him in this behalf expended, the said CAFFREY staying execution untill October next

ANDREW COCKRAN against NATHANIEL RITCHISON Defendt. In Debt

This day came the parties by their attorneys and mutually agreed to wave the Issue by the Countey and submitt the matter to the Judgment of the Court whereupon all and singular the premises being seen and by the Court now here

Page 234. Caroline County Court 10th day of August 1764

fully understood mature of deliberation being thereupon had its considered that the Plaintif recover against the Defendt. the sum of Fifty four pounds Two shillings and Seven pence and also his cost by him in this behalf expended and the said Defendant in mercy

This Judgment (except the cost) is to be discharged on payment of Seventeen pounds Fourteen shillings Ten pence Three farthings current money with Interest on Fifteen pounds Fourteen shillings three pence part thereof from the first day of February 1763 till paid

JOHN QUARLES Plaintif against GEORGE WILY Defendant On Petition

The Defendant confest Judgment to the sd Plaintif for the sum of One pound Ten shillings which he is ordered to pay with an Attorneys fee and costs

JAMES GOUGE Plaintif against JOHN PICKETT Defendant In Debt

This suit is dismissed the Plaintif paying costs

JOHN GAWITH Plaintif against BENJAMIN HUBBARD & JOHN BOWCOCK Defendts. In Debt. This day came the parties by their Attorneys who mutually agreed to wave the Issue to the Countrey and submit the matter to the Judgment of the Court whereupon all and singular the premises being seen and by the

Page 235. Caroline County Court 10th day of August 1764

Court now here fully understood mature deliberation thereupon had its considered by the Court that the Plaintif recover against the Defendants One hundred and Forty five pounds Sterling and also his cost by him in this behalf expended staying Execution till next Court then to be in mercy

This Judgment (except the cost) is to be discharged on payment of Seventy two pounds Fifteen shillings Sterling with Interest thereon to be computed after the rate of five percent per annum from the Seventeenth day of August One thousand seven hundred and Sixty two until the same is fully paid

JAMES JOHNSTON Plaintif againt PHILLIP MAY Defendant Trespass on the Case This day came as well the said JAMES by his Attorney as the said PHILLIP by his Attorney and the Jurrors of a Jury to wit JOHN NORMENT foreman etc who to say the truth of the premises being elected tried & sworn upon their oath do say that the said Defendt. is no ways guilty of the premises charged upon him by the said Plaintif as the said Defendt. in pleading hath alledged therefore its considered by the Justices here that the said Plaintif take nothing by his Bill aforesd but for his false clamour be in mercy and that the said Defendant go thereof without day and further by the Justices its here considered that the said Defendt. recover agt. the sd Plt. his cost by him about his Defence in this behalf expended and the sd Deft. have thereof execution

Page 236. Caroline County Court 10th day of August 1764

WILLIAM MULLIN Plaintif against JOHN WILY Defendant Trespass on the case This day came the parties by their attorneys who mutually agreed to wave the Issue by the County and submit the matter to the Judgment of the Court whereupon all and singular the premises being seen and by the Court fully understood its considered that the Plt recover against the Defendant the sum of Twenty three pounds Twelve shillings and also his cost by him in this behalf expended and the said Defendt. in mercy

REUBEN ROYSTON against AMBROSE TOOMBS Defendant in Trespass This day came the parties by their attorneys and also came the Jurors of a Jury to wit GEORGE BUCKNER foreman who to say the truth of the premises being elected tried and sworn upon their oath do say that the said Defendant is guilty of the trespass in the declaration mentioned in manner and form as the said Plaintif against him hath complained and do assess the damge of the Plaintif by reason thereof to Fifteen shillings, therefore its considered by the Justices here that the said Plt. recover against the said Defendant the aforesaid sum of Fifteen shillings damages by the Jurors aforesaid in form aforesaid assessed and further by the Justices here its considered that the said Plaintif recover against the Defendant his cost by him in this behalf expended and the said Defendt. may be taken

Page 237. Caroline County Court 10th day of August 1764

HARRY BEVERLEY Plaintif against CALEB LINDSEY Defendant Trespass This suit abates by the Defendts. death

JOHN TOWNSEND JUNR. Plt. against LAWRENCE SMITH Defendant On Petition The Plaintif haveing proved his demand Judgment is granted him against the Defendant for Two pounds one shilling and three pence which he is ordered to pay with costs

JOHN PRICE Plaintif against JOHN WILY Defendt. In Debt This day came as well the said Plt. by his Attorney as the said Defendant by his Attorney and the Jurors of a Jury to Wit GEORGE BUCKNER Foreman who to say the truth of the premises being elected tried and sworn upon their oath do say that the said Defendant is guilty of the premises charged upon him by the said Plaintif in manner and form as the said Plaintif against him hath complained therefore its considered by the Justices here that the sd Plaintif recover against the said Defendant Thirty pounds Current money with Interest thereon to be computed after the rate of five percent per annum from the sixth day of January one thousand seven hundred and sixty three till paid, and it is further considered by the Justices that the Plt. recover agst the Deft. his cost by him in this behalf expended and the sd Deft. in mercy

Page 238. Caroline County Court 10th day of August 1764

WILLIAM ROFF Plaintif against THOMAS PITMAN & WILLIAM BOWLER Defendts. In Debt. This day came the parties by their Attorneys who mutually agreed to wave the Issue by the Countrey and submit the matter to the Judgment of the Court whereupon all and singular the premises being seen and by the Court now here fully understood mature deliberation thereupon had its considered that the Plaintif recover against the said Defendants Three hundred & Thirty four pounds and also his cost by him in this behalf expended Staying Exe. till next Court and then the said Defendt. in mercy This Judgment (except the cost) is to be discharged on payment of Eighty eight pounds Three shillings with Interest on Eighty seven pounds Ten shillings to be computed after the rate of five percent per annum from the tenth day of May 1763 till paid

RICHARD FORTUNE acknowledged his Bill of Sale to BENJAMIN HUBBARD and JOHN ELLIOT PAINE which is ordered to be recorded

A Bill of Sale from GILPIN MOODY to BENJAMIN HUBBARD was approved by the oath of RICHARD FORTUNE and ordered to be recorded

On the motion of JOHN LYON an Evidence for PHILL. MAY at the suit of JOHNSTON he haveing attended two days its ordered that the said MAY pay him Fifty pounds of Tobacco for the same

On the motion of THOMAS PENNINGTON an evidence for JAS. JOHNSTON against MAY he haveing attended nine days and hath come and returned sixteen miles three times its therefore ordered that said JOHNSTON pay him Three hundred and Sixty nine pounds of Tobo for same

Page 239. Caroline County Court 10th day of August 1764

On the motion of JOHN HENDRICKS an evidence for JOHN WILY at the suit of PRICE he haveing attended two days and hath come and returned Twenty five miles its therefore ordered that the said WILY pay him one hundred and ninety four pounds of Tobo for the same

On the motion of GEORGE WILY an evidence for PHILLIP MAY at the suit of JOHN-STON he haveing attended five days its ordered that the said MAY pay him One hundred and Twenty five pounds of Tobacco for the same

On the motion of JOHN HILL an evidence for AMBROSE TOOMBS at the suit of ROY-STON he haveing attended six days its ordered that the said TOOMBS pay him One hundred and Fifty pounds of Tobacco for the same

On the motion of THOMAS GRIFFIN an evidence for REUBEN ROYSTON agst AM-BROSE TOOMBS he haveing attended five days its ordered that the sd ROYSTON pay him One hundred and Twenty five pounds of Tobo. for the same

On the motion of JOHN LONG an evidence for REUBEN ROYSTON against AMBROSE TOOMBS he haveing attended Eleven days its ordered that the said ROYSTON pay him Two hundred and Seventy five pounds of Tobo. for the same

THOMAS BURK Plaintif against JOHN ALLEXR. STILL Defendant On an Attach-ment. The Sherif having made return on the said Writ that executed it on Two negroes upon which Judgment is granted the Plaintif against the Defendant for Twenty pounds current money and also his cost by him in this behalf expended. This Judgment except the cost is to be discharged on payment of Eight pounds and Six pence with Interest on Seven

Page 240. Caroline County Court 10th day of August 1764

pounds Fifteen shillings and six pence from the twenty third day of January one thousand seven hundred and sixty four till paid, and its ordered that the Sherif sell one of the attached Negroes to satisfy the Plaintifs Judgment therewith and keep the overplus if any in his hands untill further order of this Court and make report

WILLIAM WHITLOCK SENR. Plt. against JOHN ALLEXR. STILL. Defendt. On an Attachment. Judgment is granted the Plaintif against the Defendant for Twenty seven pounds Nine shillings and Nine pence half penny and the cost of TAYLORs Suit against the said Defendant; therefore its considered by the Justices here that the Plaintif recover against the Defendant the aforesaid sum of money and Cost of TAYLOR Suit and also his cost by him in this behalf expended

And its ordered that the Sherif pay the Ballance of what he has in his hands of Satisfying BURKs Attmt. agt STILL and if that be not sufficient to satisfy this Judgment, to sell the other attached Negroe to satisfy the Plt. Judgment therewith and keep the overplus if any in his hands till further order of this Court and make a report

REUBEN BULLARD Plt. against JNO. ALEXR. STILL Defendt. On an Attachment Judgment is granted the Plaintif against the Defendant for the sum of Eight pounds Ten shillings current money

Page 241. Caroline County Court 10th day of August 1764

with interest thereon from the first day of February 1764 till paid which he is ordered to pay and also his cost by him in this behalf expended, and the Sherif haveing made return on the said Writ that he executed it in the hands of JOHN & GEORGE WILY and the said Garnashees appeared and being sworn declares that they have in their hands of the Defendants Estate Five pounds seven Shills. and three pence and its ordered that the Garnashees deliver the same to the said Plaintif and the ballance to be paid by the Sherif after Satisfying BURKE & WHITLOCKs Judgments and make report

ELIZABETH PEAY Plaintiff against JNO. ALEXR. STILL Defendt. Attachment Judgment is granted the Plaintif agst the Defendant for four pounds five shillings as also her costs by her in this behalf expended which is to be satisfied after the severall judgments against the said STILL heretofore recorded and its ordered that the Shf. in sale of the said Slaves allow the purchaser Credit till December the 25 next for Four pounds Five shillings and make report.

Its Ordered that PHILL. MAY pay JAMES REYNOLDS One hundred and Seventy five pounds of Tobo. for Seven days attnd. as an Evidence for him at the suit of JOHNSTON

In the Suit on the Attachment obtained by MATTHEW CRANK Plt. against JNO. ALLEXR. STILL Defendt. Judgment is granted the Plt. against the Defendt. for One pound Thirteen shillings and also his cost by him in this behalf expended and the Constable haveing returned on the said Writ that he executed it on a Cow therefore its ordered that the Sherif cause the said Cow to be sold accordg.

Page 242. Caroline County Court 10th day of August 1764

to law and the money ariseing by the said sale to go in satisfaction of the plaintifs Judgment and render the overplus to the Defendt. and make report

WILLIAM PAGE Plaintif against JOHN SMALT Defendt. On an Attachment The Sherif haveing returned on the sd Writ that he executed it in the hands of FRANCIS FLEMING and summoned him to appear as Garnashee and now at this day the said

FLEMING haveing appeared and being sworn as Garnashee declares that he has in his hands of the Defendants Estate the following goods (to wit) one Jointer one long plain one Jack plain one handsaw one tenant saw four sash quarter iron one Plow four rassing plains two augors four squares four chisels one Bricklayers Trowell one Do Jointer one chest and one Prayer Book and the said SMALT is Indebted to the Garnashee Four pounds Seven shillings and Ten pence and its ordered that the said Garnashee deliver the said attached goods to the Sherif and he be discharged, and its ordered that the Sherif cause the said goods to be sold according to Law, and if sufficient to satisfy the said Garnashee of the said Four pounds Seven shillings and Ten pence and return account of the same to the Court

Page 243. Caroline County Court 10th day of August 1764

HENRY BUCKHANNON Plaintif against JOHN JOHNSTON Defendant On an Attachment. The Plaintif haveing proved his demand upon which Judgment is granted the Plaintif against the Defendant for Two pounds current money and also his costs by him in this behalf expended and the said Deft. in mercy

And the Constable haveing made return on the said Atta. that he executed it on Six barrells of Corn and its ordered that the said SAMUEL the Constable deliver the same to the Sherif and its ordered that the said Sherif cause the same to be sold and the money ariseing by the said sale to go in satisfaction of the above Judgmt. and render the overplus if any to the Deft. and make report.

On the motion of JOHN KERGNEY an evidence for JOHN JOHNSTON at the suit of BUCKHANNON he haveing attended three days and hath come and returned twenty miles twice its ordered that the said JOHNSTON pay him One hundred and Ninety five pounds of Tobo. for the same

On the motion of WILLIAM EMBERSON an evidence for JOHN JOHNSTON at the suit of BUCKHANNON he haveing attended five days its ordered that the sd JOHNSTON pay him One hundred and Twenty five pounds of Tobacco for the same

Page 244. Caroline County Court 10th day of August 1764

On the motion of JOHN MITCHELL an evidence for JAMES JOHNSTON against PHILLIP MAY he haveing attended seven days and come and return Sixteen miles three times its ordered that the said JOHNSTON pay him Three hundred and Nineteen pounds of Tobo. for the same

On the motion of HARRY BEVERLEY by JOHN SEMPLE his Attorney for and Injunction in Chancery to stay proceedings at Common Law on a Judgment obtained by JOHN LINDSEY against the said BEVERLEY which Injunction is granted him, but only as to Nineteen pounds part of the said Judgment the said BEVERLEY giving Bond and Security in the Clerks Office

Ordered that the Court be adjourned till the Court in Course

EDMD. PENDLETON

At a Court held for Caroline County at the Courthouse on Thursday the Thirteenth day of September in the Fourth year of the Reign of our Sovereign Lord George the Third By the Grace of God of Great Britain France and Ireland King Defender of the Faith and so forth and in the year of our Lord MDCCLXIV

Present his Majesties Justices EDMUND PENDLETON, WILLIAM TYLER, ROBERT GILCHRIST and GABRIEL THROCKMORTON, Gentl.

A Deed of Gift for Goods and Chattles from JOHN BUCKNER to his Son PHILLIP BUCKNER was proved by the Oaths of REUBEN SAMUEL and HENRY WARE JUNR. and is admitted to record

p. 245. Caroline County Court 13th day of September 1764

JEREMIAH RAWLINGS returned an account on Oath of his Guardianship to ALBEN SEARS which account relates to the said Orphans Estate and it is ordered to be recorded

LAWRENCE TALIAFERRO Gent came into Court and Took the Oath appointed by Law and Subscribed the Test as Quarter Master

At the motion of ANTHONY SAMUEL he is allowed for Seven days attendance being sworn as an Evidence Summoned by JAMES JOHNSTON agst MAY. It is ordered that the sd JOHNSTON pay him One hundred and Seventy five pounds of Tobacco for the same as the Law directs

An Inventory and Appraisement of the Estate of CALEB LINDSEY deced being returned to the Court, it is ordered to be recorded

The Last Will and Testament of BENJAMIN ALLEN Deced being presented into Court by ERASMUS ALLEN Executor therein named and was proved by the Oath of EDWARD BROWN a witness thereto and is admitted to record

WILLIAM ALLCOCK and NICHOLAS WARE Inspectors at CONWAYS WAREHOUSE Exhibited an Account on Oath of Three thousand Nine hundred and Ninety five pounds of Tobacco which remain in their hands and which now sold at Thirteen shillings and Ten pence Current money per hundred

WILLIAM BAKER against JOHN BILLOPS on a Complaint for Freedom. The Court having heard the Complaint and the Deft. not shewing any reasonable cause for detaining him as a Servant, it is therefore considered by the Court that the sd BAKER be discharged from any further Service to the sd BILLOPS.

JAMES TAYLOR and BENJAMIN ROBINSON Gentl. are appointed to adjust the Scales and Weights at CONWAYS WAREHOUSE and also to view and examine into what repairs that will be wanting about the said WAREHOUSES

An Indenture of Bargain and Sale for land from BENJAMIN TOMPKINS to ROBERT TOMPKINS was acknowledged by the said BENJAMIN and is ordered to be recorded

JOSHUA LINDSEY Guardian of the Orphans of THOMAS JACKSON deced rendered an account on Oath of the said LINDSEYs Guardianship etc. and the same is ordered to be recorded

Page 246. Caroline County Court 13th day of September 1764

On the Petition of JOHN ALMAND, CARR McGEHEE and GARRETT HACKETT praying for Counter Security or otherwise from JOHN WATTS in relation to the Estate of the Orphans of THOMAS HEWLETT deced, It is ordered that he be summoned to the next Court

On the motion of GEORGE YATES to have liberty to Turn the road from GUINEYS's BRIDGE by his Plantation, It is ordered that JOHN GRIFFIN, WILLIAM ROGERS, THOMAS SCOTT and BENJAMIN TOMPKINS or any three of them being first sworn before some Justice of this County, do view the way proposed by the said GEORGE YATES and report to the Court the Conveniences and Inconveniences attending the same

ROBERT GILCHRIST and LUNSFORD LOMAX JUNR. Gentl. are appointed to adjust the Scales and Weights at ROYS WAREHOUSE

An Indenture of Bargaine and Sale between GEORGE EVANS and MARY his Wife and CHRISTIAN EVANS their Mother and JOHN ELLIOT PAINE with a Receipt thereon was acknowledged by the sd GEORGE and MARY she being first privately examined, and the sd CHRISTIAN's part was proved to be her act and deed by the Oath of BENJAMIN HUBBARD & THOMAS POLLARD two of the witnesses thereto and is admitted to record

Ordered that the CHURCHWARDENS of the Parish of St. Margaret bind out ELISHA and BENJAMIN ESTES Orphans of ABRAHAM ESTES deced according to Law

On the Petition of JOHN NORMENT it is ordered that JOHN TAYLOR gent. and JEREMIAH RAWLINGS JUNR. do settle a further account of the Guardianship of PRECILLA NORMENT an Orphan and return their settlement to Court

JAMES JAMESON and RICHARD ROY Inspectors at ROYS WAREHOUSE Exhibited an Account on Oath of Three thousand Two hundred and Forty one pounds of tobacco which remain in their hands and which now sold to JOHN SUTTON at Thirteen shillings & Eleven pence current money per hundred

On the motion of GEORGE YATES by his Attorney, it is ordered that Execution issue according to the Act of Assembly against JOHN WILY and JOHN SUTTON according to a former Judgment and Execution.

On the motion of EDWARD POWERS by his Attorney, it is ordered that Execution issue according to Act of Assembly against LUNSFORD LOMAX JUNR. according to a former Judgment and Execution

Page 247. Caroline County Court 13th day of September 1764

An Indenture for Land with a Receipt thereon from GEORGE BROOKE Gent and ANN his Wife to JOHN JONES was proved to be the act and deed of the said GEORGE by JOHN MILLER, WILLIAM HARRISON and THOMAS LAUGHLIN three of the witnesses thereto and the sd ANN having conveyed her Right by Virtue of a Commision for her Examination the same is admitted to record

Also an Indenture for Land with a receipt thereon from the same persons to JOHN THILMAN was proved as above etc. and is admitted to record

ELLINOR BABER Orphan of EDWARD BABER Deced came into Court and by the Consent of the Court Chused FRANCIS BABER her Guardian who gave Bond according to Law

A Deed of Sale for Sundry goods and Chattells from GIPPIN MOODY to BENJAMIN HUBBARD Gent was further proved by the Oath of JOHN ELLIOT PAIN and is Ordered to be recorded

WILLIAM WOODFORD, WALKER TALIAFERRO, JAMES MILLER, JOHN BUCKNER, WILLIAM BUCKNER and THOMAS LOWERY Gentlemen are by the Court recommended to the Governor as persons Quallified which are desired to be added to the Commission of the Peace for this County, And it is likewise represented to his Honour that LUNSFORD LOMAX, JOHN BAYLOR, RICHARD BUCKNER, JOHN SUTTON and LAWRENCE TALIAFERRO Gentl. do refuse to serve as Justices for this County

SAMUEL SALE an Orphan came into Court and Chused WILLIAM HOARD his Guardian who gave bond according to Law

Deeds of Lease and release for Land from THOMAS WALKER Gent. and MILDRED his Wife to WALKER TALIAFERRO was proved to be the Act and Deed of the said THOMAS by JOHN BAYLOR, ANTHONY THORNTON, and OLLIVER TOWLES JUNR. Gent. three of the witnsses to the sd Deeds and the sd MILDRED having acknowledged her part by Virtue of a Commission, the same are admitted to record

A Deed from ROBERT BEVERLEY and Others to ROBERT GILCHRIST Gent. was acknowledged by EDWARD DIXON, OLLIVER TOWLES and GILCHRIST and the sd BEVERLEY part was proved by the Oaths of RICHARD ROY and JOHN GRAY two of the Witnesses to the said Deed and is ordered to be Certified

At the motion of SIMON MILLER he is allowed for Seven days attendance as an Evidence summoned by HARRY BEVERLEY agt. WHITE. It is ordered that the sd BEVERLEY pay him One hundred and Seventy five pounds of Tobacco for the same as the Law directs

Page 248. Caroline County Court 13th day of September 1764

BENJAMIN WINN Guardian to MARY and DOLLY DURRETT Orphans returned an account on Oath of the said Orphans Estate which is ordered to be recorded

JAMES RIDDLE Guardian to WILLIAM DURRETT an Orphan also rendered an account on Oath which is ordered to be Certified & recorded

RICHARD DURRETT as Guardian to JOEL DURRETT an Orphan also rendered an account on Oath, Ordered to be recorded

Absent EDMUND PENDLETON Gent.

The Executors of JAMES TAYLOR Deced Complts. }
against } In Chancery
WILLIAM BOWLER Defendant }

This day came the parties by their attornies and the auditors report being returned in these words: Pursuant to an order of Caroline Court appearing Intricate and Difficult to be settled in Dispute between the partys which Trouble offered to pay the sum of Ten pounds and costs, which the Plaintiffs considering the Uncertainty of the Demand agreed to accept of which at their request we Certifie this 12th day of July 1764. BAYLOR WILLIAM BUCKNER, FRANCIS COLEMAN. Whereupon it is Directed by this Court that the Complainants recover of the Defendant Ten pounds current money and their costs in this suit expended, all which is the Decree of this Court in this Cause

Ordered that the Court be adjourned till to Morrow Morning Nine of the Clock

The minutes of these proceedings were signed by ROBERT GILCHRIST

At a Court continued and held for Caroline County on Friday September the 14th 1764 Present His Majesties Justices EDMUND PENDLETON, ROBERT GILCHRIST, WILLIAM PARKER, JOHN TAYLOR & GABRIEL THROCKMORTON, Gentlemen

ANN JONES Admrx. etc. Plt. agst. JOHN TOWNSEND JUNR. & JAMES DYGARNETT Defts. By Petition. This suit is dismissed

Page 249. Caroline County Court 14th day of September 1764

ROBERT GARROT Plt. agst. PEYTON SMITH Deft. In Debt

This day came the parties by their Attornies and the Defendant put in his plea and time is given the Plt to consider the same

HENRY PEMBERTON Plt. agst JOHN BILLOPS Deft. In Debt

This day came the Plt by his Attorney and the Defendt. failing to appear when called, It is considered that the Plts. Damages be Inquired into by a Jury at the next Court

HENRY RITCHIE Plt. agst. BENJAMIN HUBBARD & Others Defts. In Debt

This day came the Plt. by his Attorney and the Defendants Plead payment to which the Plt. replied and Joyned Issue and the Tryal thereof is referred till the next Court

ROBERT ROBERTS Plt. agst RICHARD STRAUGHN Deft. By Petition

This day came the Plt. and the Defendant also appeared, and the Plt. having proved his account for Four pounds Eleven shillings and Nine pence Current money, it is considered by the Court that he recover of the Defendt. the same and his costs in this Suit expended and the sd Deft. in mercy etc.

WILLIAM CUNNINGHAM etc. Plt. agst. JOHN POLLETT Defendt. In Case
This day came the Plts by their Attorney and the Defendt. being Solemnly called came not and the Sherif having returned on the Attachment Executed, therefore it is ordered that the Sherif impannel a Jury to Come before the next Court to Inquire thereof

JAMES GEORGE Plt. agst JEREMIAH JORDAN Deft. In Debt
This Suit is continued and Ordered that a summons do issue for JOHN SUTTON Gent. late Sherif to shew cause why the Plts. Writ was not executed

ROBERT ROBERTS Plt. agst. REUBEN STRAUGHN Deft. By Petition
This Suit is dismist it being not executed

JOHN PICKETT Plt. agst GEORGE TRIBLE Deft. In Case
This day came the Plt by his Attorney and

Page 250. Caroline County Court 14th September 1764

the Sherif having returned on the Plurias Capias (blurred) motion of the Plt. an Attachment against the said Defendants Estate is granted him

ARCHIBALD McCALL Plt. against JOHN WILY Defendt. In Debt
This day came the Plaintiff by his Attorney and the Defendant being again Solemnly called came not but made Default Therefore it is considered by the Court that the Plt recover against the said Defendant and WILLIAM PARKER Gent. his Security Thirty pounds Thirteen shillings and a half penny current money and his costs in this suit Expended, but This Judgment is to be discharged by the paiment of Nine pounds Eight shillings and Two pence three Farthings current money together with lawfull Interest thereon from the Sixteenth day of July 1762 until paid and the costs of this suit

JOHN WATKINS Plt. agst. WILLIAM JOHNSTON JUNR. and WILLIAM CHICK Deft. In Detinue. This day came the Parties by their attornies and the Defendant plead that they do not detain to which the Plt. replied and joyned Issue and the Trial thereof is referred to the next Court

JOHN and WILLIAM McCALL Plt. against JOHN WILY Defendant In Debt
This day came the Plts. by their attorney and the Defendant being again Solemnly called came not but made default, Therefore it is considered by the Court that the Plt recover against the said Defendant and WILLIAM PARKER Gent his Security Twenty Two pounds Nine shillings current money and their costs in this suit expended and the Defendant and Secuirty in Mercy etc., But this Judgment is to be discharged by the paiment of Eleven pounds Four shillings and Five pence current money together with Lawfull Interest thereon from the Eleventh day of August 1763 untill paid and the costs of this Suit

WILLIAM CUNNINGHAM & COMPANY Plt. against JOHN ASHBURN JUNR. Deft. In Debt. This day came the Plts. by their Attorney and the Sherif having returned on the plurias capias Copy left on the motion of the Plt. an Attachment against the Defts. Estate is granted him

JOHN and WILLIAM McCALL ass. etc. Plt. against ROBERT CHAPMAN Defendant In Debt. This day came the Plt by his Attorney and the

Page 251. Caroline County Court 14th day of September 1764

Defendant being solemnly called came not, and the Sherif having returned on the Attachment granted in this Suit that he had attached one large Trunk and two feather Beds and furniture, It is considered by the Court that the Plaintiff recover of the Defendant Nine pounds Ten shillings current money and his costs in this suit expended and It is ordered that the Sherif sell at Public Auction the goods by him Attacht and pay the

Plaintiffs their Debt and costs and the Overplus, if any, to be returned to the Defendant

ARCHIBALD McCALL and COMPANY Plt. against JACOB VAUGHAN Defendant In Trespass upon the Case. This day came the Plts by their attorney and the Defendant being solemnly called came not, Therefore it is considered by the Court that the Plaintiffs recover of the Defendt. and RACHEL VAUGHAN his Security for their Damages, But because the sd Damages are unknown to the Court Therefore it is Ordered that the Sherif summon a Jury to come before the next Court to inquire thereof

JAMES TERRELL & CARR McGEHEE Plt. agst. JAMES FARISH Defendant In Debt This day came the Plts by their Attorney and the Defendt. failing to appear It is considered by the Court that the Plt. recover of the Defendant their costs in this suit expended and the Defendant in Mercy etc.

JOHN SEMPLE Surviving Partner etc Plt. agst. WILLIAM CHEWNING Defendant By Petition. This day came the Plaintiff and the Defendant failing to appear, It is therefore considered by the Court that the Plaintiff recover of the Defendent One pound Nineteen shillings and One penny current money with an attorney fee and his costs in this suit expended and the said Defendant in Mercy etc.

STEPHEN LOW Plt. agst. THOMAS BURCH Deft. In Case This day came the parties and this suit is continued for the Auditors to return their report.

WILLIAM MOTHLEY Plt. agst. MARK MARRIOTTE Defendt. In Debt This day came the Plaintiff by his Attorney and the Defendant tho solemnly called came not And the Sherif having returned on an Attachment granted in this Suit That he had attached One spoon of the Defendants Estate, It is considered by the Court that the Plaintiff recover of the Defendant

Page 252. Caroline County Court 14th day of September 1764

Eight pounds Seventeen shillings and Four pence current money and his costs in this Suit expended and the said Defendant in Mercy etc., And it is ordered that the Sherif shall sell at public auction as the Law directs the goods by him attacht and Satisfy and pay the Plt. what the sale may amount to and make return of his proceedings therein

HARRY BEVERLEY Esqr. Plt. against RICHARD ALCOCK Defendt. By Writ of Wright. This day came the parties by their Attornies and the Defendant put in his plea and time is given the Plt. to consider the same

The Same Plaintiff against JOHN BOUTWELL Defendt. By Writ of Right This day came the parties by their attornies and the Defendt. put in his Plea and time is given the Plt. to consider the same

DILLARD HARRIS Plaintiff against WILLIAM WATTS JUNR. Deft. By Attachment This Suit is continued

WILLIAM RICHESON Plaintiff against RICHARD ROW Defendant By Attachment This day came the parties by their Attornies and further time is given the Plaintiff to reply

WILLIAM SPILLER Plt. agst. LAZARUS YARBROUGH Deft. In Debt This day came the parties by their Attorneys and the Defendt. being Solemnly called came not and the Sherif having returned on the plurias capias not found on motion of the Plt an Attachment against the Defts. Estate is granted him

WILLIAM HUBANK Plt. agst. JAMES SOUTHWORTH Deft. In Trespass This day came the Plaintiff by his Attorney and the Defendant being solemnly called came not, Therefore it is considered by the Court that unless the Defendt. appear here at the next Court and answer the Plts. action that Judgment will then be given the Plt. against the said Defendt. for his Damages.

Page 253. Caroline County Court 14th day of September 1764

JOHN YOUNGER Mercht. Plt. agst. DAVID STERN Defendt. In Case
This day came the parties by their Attornies and this Suit is continued for the Audit-tors to return their Report

BENJAMIN ROWE Plt. agst. FRANCIS FLEMING Deft. In Debt
This suit is dismist.

JOHN BROWN Plt. agst WILLIAM BOWLER Deft.
This suit is continued

SIMON MILLER Plt. agst. ROBERT ROBERTS Deft. By Attachment
This suit is continued

CHARLES STORY Plt. agst WILLIAM JOHNSTON JUNR. Deft. In Case
This suit is continued for the Audittors report

JOHN SEMPLE Surviving Partner etc. Plt. agst. ROBERT HUDGENS and JOHN COLQUIT Exrs. etc. Defendts. By Attachment
This day came the Plt. and the Defendants failing to appear and the Sherif having re-turned an attachment served in the hands of ROBERT TALIAFERRO, It is Considered by the Court that the Plaintiff recover of the Defendants and ROBERT TALIAFERRO Gar-nishee the sum of Two pounds Six shillings and Three pence current money and his costs in this suit expended and the sd Defts. and Garnishee in mercy etc.

JOSEPH BROCK and EDWARD HERNDON Exrs. etc. Plaintiff agst. JOHN CANNON De-fendant. In Debt
This day came the Plts. by their attorney and the Defendant failing to appear and the Sherif having returned on the Attachments granted in this Suit that they had attached one Plate and one Broad Axe of the Defendants Estate. It is Considered by the Court that the

Page 254. Caroline County Court 14th day of September 1764

Plaintiffs recover of the Defendts. Eight pounds Sixteen shillings and Five pence Cur-rent money and their costs in this suit expended and the said Defendts. in Mercy etc., But this Judgment is to be discharged by the paiment of Four pounds Eight shillings and Two pence half penny current money together with lawfull interest thereon from the Twenty fifth day of October 1760 untill paid and the Costs of this Suit, And it is Ordered that the Sherif sell the goods by him Attacht at Auction as the Law directs and pay the Plts. what the sale may amount to towards discharging their Debts & costs and return his proceedings therein

JOHN SEMPLE Surviving Partner of ROBERT BAYLOR Gent. Deced Plaintiff agst JOHN ASHBURN Defendant. In Debt
This day came the Plaintiff and the Defendant tho solemnly called came not, And the Sherif having returned on the Attachment granted in this Suit that he had attached One feather bed and furniture of the Defendants Estate, It is therefore considered by the Court that the Plaintiff recover of the Defendt. Nine pounds Thirteen shillings and One penny farthing Current money and his costs in this suit expended and the said Defendt. in Mercy etc., But this Judgment is to be discharged by the paiment of Four pounds Sixteen shillings and Six pence three farthings current money and the costs of this suit with Interest from the Second of November 1761 untill paid And it is Ordered that the Sherif sell the goods by him Attacht at auction as the Law directs and Satisfie and pay what the sale may amount to to the Plt. towards discharging his Debt and costs and make return of his proceedings therein

JOHN ROSE etc. Plaintiff agst. JOHN GEORGE Defendt. In Debt
This day came the Plts. by their Attorney and the Defendant tho solemnly called came not Therefore it is Considered by the Court that unless the Defendt. appear here at the next Court and answer the Plaintiffs action that Judgment will then be given to the Plts. against the Defendant and JOHN GEORGE SENR. his Security for the Plaintiffs Debt and costs.

Page 255. Caroline County Court 14th day of September 1764

JOHN ORR and THOMAS HODGE Plt. agst. ROBERT TURNBULL Defendant. In Debt
This day came the Plaintiffs by their Attorney and the Defendant tho Solemnly called came not and it appearing to the Court that Seven pounds Five shillings and Three pence Current money is due to the Plaintiffs, Therefore it is Considered by the Court that the Plaintiffs recover against the sd Defendant the sum (   ) with interest from 17th day of November 1761 being part thereof and their costs in this suit expended and the sd Deft. in Mercy etc. And it is Ordered that MARY TALIAFERRO deliver to the Sherif Sixty six pounds of Tobacco to be by him sold as the Law directs and the money arising by such sale to be paid to the Plts. towards discharging their Debt and costs and that he make return of his proceedings therein

WILLIAM JOHNSTON Plaintiff against JAMES FARISH Defendant In Trespass upon the Case. This day came the Plaintiff by his Attorney and the Defendant failing to appear when called and the Audittors report being returned in these words: We the Subscribers viewed the Damages shown to us by Capt. WM. JOHNSTON which he affirmed to us was done to him by JAMES FARISH and we have valued the same to Two pounds Ten shillings and Six pence. Given under our hands this 14th day of December 1762 JOHN WILY, GEORGE WILY. It is therefore considered by the Court that the Plaintiff recover against the Defendant the Damages by the Audittors assessed and his costs in this suit expended and the said Defendant in mercy etc.

On the petition of the REVEREND ARCHIBALD DICK to have a liberty to Turn a Road leading to PULLIAMs FORD, It is ordered that WILLIAM TYLER, GABRIEL THROCKMORTON Gentl. CHRISTOPHER TOMPKINS and JOHN CLARK or any three of them being first sworn before some Justice of the peace of this County do view the said way and Report the Conveniences and Inconveniences attending the same to the Court

Page 256. Caroline County Court 14th day of September 1764

JOHN TURNER Plaintiff agst. JOHN TOWNSEND SENR. Deft. In Debt
This day came the Parties by their Attornies and the Defendant put in his special Demurrer which the Plaintiff joyned and the same is referred till the next Court for Argument

JOHN THILMAN Plaintiff agst. JOHN ASHBURN Defendt. In Debt
This day came the Plaintiff by his Attorney and the Defendt. tho solemnly called came not and the Sherif having returned on the Attachment granted in this Suit that he had attached one feather bed and furniture, It is Therefore considered by the Court that the Plaintiff recover against the sd Defendant Five pounds Five shillings current money and his costs in this suit expended and the sd Defendant is Mercy etc. And it is ordered that the Sherif sell at public auction the goods by him attacht and Satisfie and pay the Plt his Debt and costs and the overplus, if any, he return to the Defendt. and make return of his proceedings therein

ARCHIBALD INGRAM and GEORGE KIPPEN Plt. agst. JOHN POWELL Defendant In Debt. This day came the Plaintiffs by their Attorney and the Defendant tho solemnly called came not and the Sherif having returned on the Attachment granted in this Suit that he had attached One Broad Hoe of the Defendants Estate, It is therefore considered by the Court that the Plts. recover against the Defendant Thirty three pounds current money and their costs in this Suit expended and the said Defendant in Mercy etc. But the same is to be discharged by the paiment of Fifteen pounds Eight shillings and three pence half penny current money together with Lawful Interest thereon from the Month of October 1762 untill paid and the costs of this suit And it is Ordered that the Sherif sell at Public Auction the goods by him attacht and pay to the Plt. what the Sale may amount to towards discharging his Debt and costs and make return of his proceedings therein

FRANCIS SMITH Plaintiff agst. FRANCIS FLEMING Defendt. In Case
This day came the Plt. by his Attorney and the Deft. also appeared and pleads Non assumpsit which the Plt Joyned and the Trial thereof is referred till the next Court, And JOHN ELLIOTT PAIN Security for the Defendants appearance came into Court and

Page 257. Caroline County Court 14th September 1764

surrendered him up and the Court are of the opinion he had a right to do so which the Plaintiff objected to and refused to pray him in Custody

PHILLIP MAY Assignee Etc. Plt. against WILLIAM WALLER Defendt. In Debt
This day came the parties by their Attornies and this Suit is referred till the next Court for Argument on the Plea Replication Demurrer and Joynder

SAMUEL BOSWORTH etc. Mercht. in London Plt. agst. LUNSFORD LOMAX Gent Defendt. In Debt. This day came the parties by their attornies and JOHN LEWIS entered himself Security for the Costs of suit and the Defendt. Pleads that he owes nothing to which the Plaintiff replied and Joyned Issue and the Trial thereof is referred till the next Court

JOHN BROWN Plt. agst. RICHARD JOHNSTON Deft. In Case
This day came the parties by their attornies and the Defendt. pleads Non Assumpsit to which the Plt. replied and joyned Issue and the Trial thereof is referred till the next Court

ROBERT GILCHRIST gent Plt. agst. ACHILLES WHITLOCK Defendt. By Attachment
This day came the Plaintiff and the Defendant being solemnly called came not and it appearing that Three pounds Nine shillings and Seven pence current money is due to the Plt., Therefore it is Considered by the Court that the Plt. recover of the Defendant the same and his costs in this suit expended and the said Defendant in Mercy etc. And it is Ordered that JOHN TURNER the Garnishee pay the Plt. Two pounds Five shillings and One penny current money in part of his Debt and Costs

ANDREW ANDERSON Plt. against THOMAS CROMPTON Deft. In Debt
This day came the Plt. by his Attorney And it appearing that Twenty pounds Current money is due by Bond to the Plt. It is Therefore considered by the Court that the Plt recover of the Defendant the same and his costs in this Suit expended and the said Defendt. in Mercy etc., but this Judgment is to be discharged by the paiment of Nine pounds Nineteen shillings and Eight pence half penny Currt. money with lawfull interest thereon from the first day of November 1763 untill paid and the costs of this suit

Page 258. Caroline County Court 14th September 1764

EDWARD DIXON etc. Plt. agst. JAMES GOUGE and SIMON MILLER Defendts. In Debt
This day came the parties by their Attornies and the Defendt. pleads payment to which the Plt. replied and Joyned Issue and the Trial thereof is referred till the next Court

JOHN BACKHOUSE Mercht. Plt. agst. HARRY BEVERLEY Gent. Defendt. In Case
This day came the parties by their attornies and the Defendt. pleads Non Assumpsit to which the Plt replied and Joyned Issue and the Trial thereof is referred till the next Court

WILLIAM and FRANCIS BICKLEY Plt. agst. DAVID DAVENPORT and JOHN MEACHAM Defts. In Debt.
This day came the Plts by their Attorney and the Defendts. tho solemnly called came not Therefore it is considered that unless the Defendt. MEACHAM appear here at the next Court and answer the Plts. action that Judgment will then be granted the Plts. agst. the sd MEACHAM and JOHN ELLIOT PAYNE his Security for the Plaintiffs Debt and costs

The Last Will and Testament of MUSGROVE DAWSON Deced was proved by the Oath of MARY GRIMES a Witness thereto and Sworn to in Court by MARY DAWSON Executrix therein named and Ordered to be recorded and on motion of the sd Exx. Certificate is granted her for obtaining a probate thereof in due form she having given bond and acknowledged the same in Court

Ordered that GEORGE TAYLOR, WILLIAM ALLOCK, SETH THORNTON and WILLIAM WOODFORD Gentl. or any three of them being first sworn before a Justice of this County do appraise in current money the Slaves and personal Estate of MUSGROVE DAWSON Deced and return the Appraisement to the Court

GEORGE WILY Plt. agst. JOHN WATKINS Deft. By Attachment
This Suit is continued

ISROM COGHILL Plt. agst. JOHN WATKINS Deft. By Attachment
This Suit is continued

ROBERT ROBERTS Plaintiff against PHILLIP MAY Defendant By Petition
This day came the parties and the Court having fully heard the Issue are of the Oppinion that One pound Fourteen shillings and Ten pence current money is due to the Plaintiff It is therefore considered that the Plt. recover of the Defendant the same and his costs in this suit expended and the said Defendant in Mercy etc.

Page 259. Caroline County Court 14th day of September 1764

ROBERT ROBERTS Plt. agst. JOHN BOWCOCK Deft. By Petition
This day came the Plt. and it appearing tht Three pounds Nineteen shillings and Seven pence current money is due to him from the Defendt. Therefore it is considered by the Court that the Plaintiff recover against the sd Defendant the same and his costs in this suit expended and the sd Defendant in Mercy etc.

JOHN FALKNER Plt. agst. JOHN WILEY Defendt. In Debt
This day came the parties by their attornies and WILLIAM PARKER Gent entered himself special bail for the Defendt. who pleads payment to which the Plt. replied and joyned Issue and the trial thereof is referred till the next Court

On the motion of JOHN PICKETT for Counter Security from JOSEPH REYNOLDS and his Wife as Exr. and Exx. of ABRAHAM ESTES deced, By consent of the sd REYNOLDS and Wife ANTHONY THORNTON gent is appointed Guardian for this Purpose to Act in behalf of the Deceds Children and it is ordered that WILLIAM BUCKNER, ROBERT TALIAFERRO and GABRIEL THROCKMORTON Gentl. or any two of them do settle the accounts of the Administrations the profits of the Estate and the Maintenance of the Children and to Divide the same according to the Will of the Deced and to make their report to the Court

WILLIAM COCK Plt. agst. THOMAS BOOTH Deft. In case
This day came the Plaintiff by his Attorney andthe Defendt. failing to appear when called, It is therefore considered by the Court that the Plaintiff recover against the said Defendt. his Damages But because they are unknown to the Court therefore It is ordered

that the Sherif Impannell a Jury to come before the Next Court to Inquire thereof

ANNE TAYLOR Plt. against JOHN ELLIOTT PAINE Defendt. In Case
This day came the parties by their Attornies and the Deft. pleads not Guilty to which the Plt. replied and Joyned Issue and the Trial thereof is referred till the next Court

FRANCIS TAYLOR Ass: Etc. Plt. agst. JOHN BOWCOCKand GEORGE WILY Defendts. In Debt. This suit is referred to EDMUND PENDLETON Gent to arbitrate and after giving legal notice he is to proceed Ex partie

Page 260. Caroline County Court 14th day of September 1764

WILLIAM HARRISON Plaintiff against JAMES JOHNSTON Defendt. In Case
This day came the Plaintiff by his Attorney and the Defendt. being again solemnly called came not but made Default, Therefore it is considered by the Court that the Plt. recover of the Defendant and FRANCIS COLEMAN his Security his Damages, But Becauise these Damages are unknown to the Court Therefore it is ordered that the Sherif summon a Jury to come before the next Court to Inquire thereof

ANDREW COCKRAN and COMPA. Plt. agst. JOHN PAGE Defendt. In Case
This day came the Plts.by their attorney and the Defendant tho solemnly called came not Therefore it is considered by the Court that unless the Defendant appear here at the next Court and Answer the Plts. action that Judgment will then be given him against the sd Defendt. and WILLIAM PAGE his Security for the Plts. damages

THE SAME PLT. agst. JOHN BOWCOCK Defendt. In Debt
This day came the parties and the Defendant in Custody of the Sherif pleads payment which the Plt. Joyned and the Trial thereof if referred till the next Court

JOHN PITTS Plt. agst. THOMAS HEATH Defendt. In Case
This day came the parties by their Attornies and the Defendt. pleads Non Assumpsit which the Plt. Joyned and the Trial thereof is referred till the next Court

JOHN BOWCOCK Plt. agst. FRANCIS TAYLOR Gent. Defendt. In Case
This day came the parties by Consent this suit is referred to EDMUND PENDLETON Gent to Arbitrate and after legal Notice given he is to proceed Ex Partie

BENJAMIN HUBBARD Plt. agst. WILLIAM EDLINGTON Deft. By Scire facias
This day came the Plt. by his Attorney and the Defendt. tho solemnly called came not and the Sherif having returned that he is not found, It is therefore considered by the Court that Judgment be renewed for Five pounds Eighteen shillings and Eight pence current money Fifteen Shillings or One hundred and Fifty pounds of tobacco also Eighty seven pounds of tobacco and the costs of this suit and that Execution thereon be awarded.

Page 261. Caroline County Court 14th day of September 1764

JOHN RICHARDS Gent. Plt. agst THOMAS RIDDLE SENR. Deft. In Case
This day came the Plaintiff by his Attorney and the Defendant tho solemnly called came not and the Sherif having attacht some of the Defendants Estate Therefore it is Ordered that he Impannell a Jury to come before the next Court to Inquire into the Plts. Damages

ROBERT GILCHRIST Plaintiff against LAWRENCE CATTLETT Deft. In Case
This suit is continued

WILLIAM AYRES Assignee of JOHN SUTTON Gent. Plt. agst. PETER LANTER and JOHN BOWCOCK Defendt. In Debt.
This day came the parties by their attornies and the Issue in this suit being waved and the Cause submitted to the Court, It is considered by the Court that the Plaintiff recover

against the said Defendants Fifty five pounds Twelve shillings and Eight pence Current money and his costs in this suit expended and the said Defendants in Mercy etc. But this Judgment is to be discharged by the paiment of Twenty pounds current money with Interest thereon from the 10th day of August 1763 till paid Fifteen shillings and One hundred Twenty nine pounds of Nett tobacco Twenty six shillings and Six pence and the Prison Fees together with the costs of this Suit

ABRAHAM HARPER Plaintiff agst RICHARD DURRETTE JUNR. Deft. In Trespass This day came the parties by their attornies and thereupon came also a Jury by Name JOHN GARNETT etc. who being Elected tried and sworn the truth to Speak upon the Issue Joyned upon their Oath do say That the Defendant is Guilty as the Plaintiff against him hath Complained and Do assess the Plaintiffs Damages by Occasion of the Trespass committed to Fifteen pounds Current money besides his cost. It is Therefore considered by the Court that the Plaintiff recover of the Defendant the Damages by the Jurors in their Verdict assessed and his costs in this suit Expended and the Defendt. be thereof in Mercy

JOHN FOSTER Plaintiff against JOHN ELLIOTT PAINE Deft. By Scirefacias This day came the parties by their attornies and the Defendant pleads payment to which the Plaintiff replied and Joyned Issue and the Trial thereof is referred till the next Court

Page 262. Caroline County Court 14th day of September 1764

JOHN FOSTER Plaintiff agst THOMAS BOOTH Defendt. By Scirefacias This day came the parties by their attornies and the Defendt. pleads payment to which the Plt. replied and Joyned Issue and the Trial thereof is referred till the next Court

HENRY RITCHIE Plt. agst. BENJAMIN HUBBARD & Others Defts. By Scirefacias This day came the parties by their attornies and the Defendts. Pleads payment which the Plaintiff Joyned and the Trial thereof is referred till the next Court

WILLIAM WINSTON Plt. agst WILLIAM BOWLER Deft. In Case This Suit is continued for the auditors report

BRYAN FITZPATRICK Complt. agst ANN SANDERS Admrx. etc. Defendt. In Chancery. This suit is continued for the Complts. Bill

ROBERT GILCHRIST Plt. agst SAMUEL LONG Defendt. In Case This day came the Plt. and the Defendant tho solemnly called came not, and the Sherif having returned on the Attachment that he had attached an Old Bed of the Defts. Estate therefore it is considered that the Plt. recover of the Defendant his Damages But because they are unknown to the Court it is Ordered that the Sherif summon a Jury to come before the next Court to Inquire thereof

DANIEL THILMAN Plt. agst WILLIAM EMBERSON Defendt. In Slander This suit is continued

ANDREW COCKRAN & COMPANY Plt. agst THOMAS JONES Defendt. In Debt This Day came the parties by their attornies and the Defendant pleads payment to which the Plaintiff replied and Joyned Issue and the Trial thereof is referred till the next Court

JAMES SUMMERS Plt. agst. JOHN BRAND Defendt. In Assault & Battery This suit is continued for the Plaintiff

PETER COPELAND etc. Plt. agst WILLIAM BOWLER Defendt. In Case This suit is continued for the Auditors report

Page 263. Caroline County Court 14th day of September 1764

ROBERT ROBERTS Plaintiff agst. THOMAS PITMAN Defendt. In Case

This day came the Parties by their attornies and Thereupon came a Jury by Name BENJAMIN WINN etc. who being Elected tried and sworn the truth to speak upon the Issue Joyned upon they Oath do say that the Defendt. did assume in manner and form as the Plt. against him hath Declared and do assess the Plts. Damages by Occasion of the Non performance of his Assumption to Six pounds Eighteen shillings and Three pence current money besides his Costs, it is therefore considered by the Court that the Plt. recover of the Defendant the same and his costs in this suit expended and the sd Defendant in Mercy etc.

ROBERT ROBERTS Plt. agst. GEORGE KENNER Defendt. In Case

This suit is continued for the Defendt.

ROBERT ROBERTS Plt. agst. JAMES TALIAFERRO Defendt. In Case

This day came the parties by their attornies and thereupon the issue was waved and the matter fully heard and It is considered by the Court that Six pounds eighteen shillings and three pence half penny Current money is due to the Plaintiff and that he recover of the Defendant the same and his costs in this Suit expended and that the Defendant be thereof in Mercy etc.

JAMES GILDART Esqr. Plt. agst. JAMES DISMUKES Deft. In Case

This suit is continued

ROGER DIXON Plt agst NICHOLAS OLLIVER Defendt. In Case

This suit is dismissed

JOHN CARNALL Plt. agst. MOZA HURT Defendt. By Attachment

This day came the parties and the issue being waved and submitted to the Court, who having fully heard the same are of the opinion that One pound Seventeen shillings and three pence current money is due to the Plt. therefore it is considered by the Court that the Plt. recover against the Defendant the same and his costs in this suit expended and the sd Defendt. in Mercy etc.

BENJAMIN HUBBARD Gent. Plt. agst JOHN TOWNSEND JUNR. Defendt. In Case

This day came the parties by their attornies and the Issue being waved the Audittors Report was returned, which is as follows: This suit by consent of Parties and the Order of Caroline County Court referred

Page 264. Caroline County Court 14th day of September 1764

to my Determination I have heard the parties and their witnesses, whereupon It appeared that in the Beginning of the year 1763 the Defendt. agreed to Deliver to the Plt. Fifty barrels of Corn at the price of Ten shillings a Barrel of which he only delivered Seven barrels and refused the remainder for which he ought to be accountable to the Plt. as the rate of Two shillings and Six pence a Barrel amounting to Five pounds Seven shillings and Six pence the Plt. allowing thereout Three pounds Ten shillings for the Seven barrels delivered. I do therefore award and order that the Plt. recover agst. the Defendt. Thirty seven shillings and Six pence & costs. Given under my hand August 29th 1764. EDMD. PENDLETON. It is therefore considered by the Court that the Plt. recover against the sd Defendant One pound Sixteen shillings and Six pence current money and his costs in this suit Expended and the sd Defendt. in Mercy etc.

At the motion of JOHN ELLIOT PAINE he is allowed for one days attendance as an evidence summoned by BENJAMIN HUBBARD Gent. agst. TOWNSEND JUNR. It is Ordered that the sd HUBBARD pay him Twenty five pounds of tobacco for the same as the Law directs

At the motion of JOHN PRUIT he is allowed for three days for the same agst. the same he is allowed Seventy five pounds of tobacco for his attendance

Also FRANCIS PAIN allowed for his attendance three days for the same agst the same Seventy five pounds of tobacco

Also WILLIAM PRICE allowed for his attendance three days for the same agst the same Seventy five pounds of tobacco

At the motion of GABRIEL THROCKMORTON Gent. he is allowed for Eight days attendance as an Evidence summoned by ABRAHAM HARPER against RICHARD DURRETT JUNR. It is ordered that the said HARPER pay him Two hundred pounds of tobacco for the same as the Law directs

At the motion of BENJAMIN WINN he is allowed for Eight days for the same against the same he is allowed Two hundred pounds of tobacco for his attendance

Also JOHN EDMONDSON allowed for eight days for the same agst the same allowed Two hundred pounds of Tobacco for his attendance

JOHN MILLER Plt. agst. JAMES TALIAFERRO Defendt. By Petition

This day came the Plt. and the Defendt. failing to appear It is considered by the Court that the Plt. recover of the Defendt. Three pounds fifteen shillings and four pence half penny current money and his costs in this Suit expended and the sd Defendant in Mercy etc.

DIXON agst TALIAFERRO Judgment for costs.

Page 265. Caroline County Court 14th day of September 1764

Ordered that THOMAS BOOTH serve as Overseer of the road in the room of FRANCIS FLEMING and it is Ordered that all the Tithables which served under the said FLEMING do now serve under the said BOOTH to clear and keep the said road in lawfull repair

WILLIAM JOHNSTON Plt agst. ANN TALIAFERRO & Others Exrs. etc. Defts. By Petition. This suit is dismissed it being agreed the Defendants paying costs

On the motion of JOHN TAYLOR it is Ordered that Execution do Issue according to the Act of the General Assembly against JOHN WILY and JOHN SUTTON for Sixty five pounds Current money fifteen shilling or One hundred and fifty pounds of tobacco and One hundred and Eighty five pounds of tobacco also three pounds Seven shillings and four pence Sherif fees according to a former Judgment and Execution

JOSEPH WOOD Gent. Plt. agst JOHN ELLIOT PAINE Defendt. In Case

This day came the plaintiff by his Attorney and the Defendant doth confess that Six pounds Current money is due to the Plt. It is therefore considered by the Court that the Plt. recover of the Defendant the same and his costs in this suit expended and the sd Defendant in Mercy etc.

JAMES SYMMONDS Plt. agst. GEORGE and JOHN WILY Defendts. On a former Judgment. On the motion of the Plt. it is Ordered that Execution do issue according to Act of Assembly against the sd Defts. for Thirty one pounds Current money fifteen Shillings or One hundred and fifty pounds of tobacco also two hundred thirty two pounds of Nett Tobacco and Interest Two pounds One shilling and ten pence half penny and One pound Fifteen shillings and Nine pence Sherif fees with interest from 10th May 1764 untill paid

ARCHIBALD McCALL Plt. agst. JOHN WILY and JOHN SUTTON Defts. On a former Judgement. On the motion ofthe Plt. it is Ordered that Execution do issue according to the Act of General Assembly against the sd Defendts. for Forty seven pounds Ten shillings Current money also Three pounds Nineteen shillings Interest from the 14th of October 1762 till the 4th of June 1764 Fifteen shillings for an Attorneys fee and One hundred and Ninety three pounds of tobacco and Two pounds thirteen shillings and Ten pence current money for the Sherif Fee with interest from 3d June 1764.

Absent EDMUND PENDLETON Gent.

Page 266. Caroline County Court 14th day of September 1764

JOHN TAYLOR Gent. Plt. agst WILLIAM BOWLER Defendt. In Case
This day came the parties by their attornies and the Defendt. Pleads Non Assumpsit to which the Plt. replied and Joyned Issue and the Trial thereof is referred till the next Court

The Same Plt. agst. JOHN NORMENT Defendt. In Case
This day came the Plt. by his Attorney and the Deft. being again solemnly called came not therefore it is considered by the Court that the Plt. recover of the Deft. and GEORGE GUY his Security his Damages but because they are unknown to the Court Therefore it is ordered that the Sherif summon a Jury to come before the next Court to Inquire thereof.

JOHN YOUNGER etc. Plt. agst. FRANCIS TALIAFERRO Deft. In Case
This day came the parties and it is considered by the Court that the Plaintiff recover of the Defendant his Costs in this suit Expended

JOHN TAYLOR Gent. Plt. agst JOHN ELLIOTT PAINE Defendt. In Debt
This day came the parties by their attornies and the Defendt. pleads payment to which the Plt. replied and Joyned Issue and the Trial thereof is referred till the next Court

Ordered that the Court be adjourned till To Morrow Morning Nine of the Clock

The Minutes of these proceedings were signed by ROBERT GILCHRIST

(Caroline County Order Book 1764-1765 continues in Part Two.)

Heritage Books by Ruth and Sam Sparacio:

Abstracts of Account Books of Edward Dixon, Merchant of Port Royal, Virginia, Volume I: 1743–1747

Abstracts of Account Books of Edward Dixon, Merchant of Port Royal, Virginia, Volume II

Albemarle County, Virginia Deed and Will Book Abstracts, 1748–1752

Albemarle County, Virginia Deed Book Abstracts, 1758–1761

Albemarle County, Virginia Deed Book Abstracts, 1761–1764

Albemarle County, Virginia Deed Book Abstracts, 1764–1768

Albemarle County, Virginia Deed Book Abstracts, 1768–1770

Albemarle County, Virginia Deed Book Abstracts, 1776–1778

Albemarle County, Virginia Deed Book Abstracts, 1778–1780

Albemarle County, Virginia Deed Book Abstracts, 1780–1783

Albemarle County, Virginia Deed Book Abstracts, 1787–1790

Albemarle County, Virginia Deed Book Abstracts, 1790–1791

Albemarle County, Virginia Deed Book Abstracts, 1791–1793

Augusta County, Virginia Land Tax Books, 1782–1788

Augusta County, Virginia Land Tax Books, 1788–1790

Amherst County, Virginia Land Tax Books, 1789–1791

Caroline County, Virginia Appeals and Land Causes, 1787–1794

Caroline County, Virginia Order Book Abstracts, 1765

Caroline County, Virginia Order Book Abstracts, 1767–1768

Caroline County, Virginia Order Book Abstracts, 1768–1770

Caroline County, Virginia Order Book Abstracts, 1770–1771

Caroline County, Virginia Order Book, 1764

Caroline County, Virginia Order Book, 1765–1767

Caroline County, Virginia Order Book, 1771–1772

Caroline County, Virginia Order Book, 1772–1773

Caroline County, Virginia Order Book, 1773

Caroline County, Virginia Order Book, 1773–1774

Caroline County, Virginia Order Book, 1774–1778

Caroline County, Virginia Order Book, 1778–1781

Caroline County, Virginia Order Book, 1781–1783

Caroline County, Virginia Order Book, 1783–1784

Caroline County, Virginia Order Book, 1784–1785

Caroline County, Virginia Order Book, 1785–1786

Caroline County, Virginia Order Book, 1786–1787

Caroline County, Virginia Order Book, 1787, Part 1

Caroline County, Virginia Order Book, 1788

Culpeper County, Virginia Deed Book Abstracts, 1795–1796

Culpeper County, Virginia Land Tax Book, 1782–1786

Culpeper County, Virginia Land Tax Book, 1787–1789

Culpeper County, Virginia Minute Book, 1763–1764

Digest of Family Relationships, 1650–1692, from Virginia County Court Records

Digest of Family Relationships, 1720–1750, from Virginia County Court Records

Digest of Family Relationships, 1750–1763, from Virginia County Court Records

Digest of Family Relationships, 1764–1775, from Virginia County Court Records

Essex County, Virginia Deed and Will Abstracts, 1695–1697

Essex County, Virginia Deed and Will Abstracts, 1697–1699

Essex County, Virginia Deed and Will Abstracts, 1699–1701

Essex County, Virginia Deed and Will Abstracts, 1701–1703

Essex County, Virginia Deed and Will Abstracts, 1745–1749

Essex County, Virginia Deed and Will Book, 1692–1693

Essex County, Virginia Deed and Will Book, 1693–1694

Essex County, Virginia Deed and Will Book, 1694–1695

Essex County, Virginia Deed and Will Book, 1753–1754 and 1750

Essex County, Virginia Deed Book, 1724–1728

Essex County, Virginia Deed Book, 1728–1733

Essex County, Virginia Deed Book, 1733–1738

Essex County, Virginia Deed Book, 1738–1742

Essex County, Virginia Deed Book, 1742–1745

Essex County, Virginia Deed Book, 1749–1751

Essex County, Virginia Deed Book, 1751–1753

Essex County, Virginia Land Trials Abstracts, 1711–1716 and 1715–1741

Essex County, Virginia Order Book Abstracts, 1699–1702

Essex County, Virginia Order Book Abstracts, 1716–1723, Part 1

Essex County, Virginia Order Book Abstracts, 1716–1723, Part 2

Essex County, Virginia Order Book Abstracts, 1716–1723, Part 3

Essex County, Virginia Order Book Abstracts, 1716–1723, Part 4

Essex County, Virginia Order Book Abstracts, 1723–1725, Part 1

Essex County, Virginia Order Book Abstracts, 1723–1725, Part 2

Essex County, Virginia Order Book Abstracts, 1725–1729, Part 1

Essex County, Virginia Order Book Abstracts, 1727–1729

Essex County, Virginia Order Book, 1695–1699

Fairfax County, Virginia Deed Abstracts, 1799–1800 and 1803–1804

Fairfax County, Virginia Deed Abstracts, 1804–1805

Fairfax County, Virginia Deed Book Abstracts, 1799

Fairfax County, Virginia Deed Book, 1798–1799

Fairfax County, Virginia Land Causes, 1788–1824

Fauquier County, Virginia Minute Book Abstracts, 1759–1761

Fauquier County, Virginia Minute Book Abstracts, 1761–1762

Fauquier County, Virginia Minute Book Abstracts, 1766–1767

Fauquier County, Virginia Minute Book Abstracts, 1767–1769

Fauquier County, Virginia Minute Book Abstracts, 1769–1771

Hanover County, Virginia Land Tax Book, 1782–1788

Hanover County, Virginia Land Tax Book, 1789–1793

Hanover County, Virginia Land Tax Book, 1793–1796

King George County, Virginia Order Book Abstracts, 1721–1723

King George County, Virginia Deed Book Abstracts, 1721–1735

King George County, Virginia Deed Book Abstracts, 1735–1752

King George County, Virginia Deed Book Abstracts, 1753–1773

King George County, Virginia Deed Book Abstracts, 1773–1783

King George County, Virginia Will Book Abstracts, 1752–1780

King William County, Virginia Record Book, 1702–1705

King William County, Virginia Record Book, 1705–1721

King William County, Virginia Record Book, 1722 and 1785–1786

Lancaster County, Virginia Deed and Will Book, 1652–1657

Lancaster County, Virginia Deed and Will Book, 1654–1661

Lancaster County, Virginia Deed and Will Book, 1661–1702 (1661–1666 and 1699–1702)

Lancaster County, Virginia Deed Book Abstracts, 1701–1706

Lancaster County, Virginia Deed Book, 1710–1714

Lancaster County, Virginia Order Book Abstracts, 1656–1661

Lancaster County, Virginia Order Book Abstracts, 1662–1666

Lancaster County, Virginia Order Book Abstracts, 1666–1669

Lancaster County, Virginia Order Book Abstracts, 1670–1674

Lancaster County, Virginia Order Book Abstracts, 1674–1678

Lancaster County, Virginia Order Book Abstracts, 1678–1681

Lancaster County, Virginia Order Book Abstracts, 1682–1687

Lancaster County, Virginia Order Book Abstracts, 1729–1732

Lancaster County, Virginia Order Book Abstracts, 1736–1739

Lancaster County, Virginia Order Book Abstracts, 1739–1742

Lancaster County, Virginia Order Book, 1687–1691

Lancaster County, Virginia Order Book, 1691–1695

Lancaster County, Virginia Order Book, 1695–1699

Lancaster County, Virginia Order Book, 1699–1701

Lancaster County, Virginia Order Book, 1701–1703

Lancaster County, Virginia Order Book, 1703–1706

Lancaster County, Virginia Order Book, 1732–1736

Lancaster County, Virginia Will Book, 1675–1689

Loudoun County, Virginia Order Book, 1763–1764

Loudoun County, Virginia Order Book, 1764

Louisa County, Virginia Deed Book, 1744–1746

Louisa County, Virginia Order Book, 1742–1744

Madison County, Virginia Deed Book Abstracts, 1793–1804

Madison County, Virginia Deed Book, 1793–1813, and Marriage Bonds, 1793–1800

Middlesex County, Virginia Deed Book, 1679–1688

Middlesex County, Virginia Deed Book, 1688–1694

Middlesex County, Virginia Deed Book, 1694–1703

Middlesex County, Virginia Deed Book, 1703–1709

Middlesex County, Virginia Deed Book, 1709–1720

Middlesex County, Virginia Order Book Abstracts, 1686–1690

Middlesex County, Virginia Order Book Abstracts, 1697–1700

Middlesex County, Virginia Record Book, 1721–1813

Northumberland County, Virginia Deed and Will Book, 1650–1655

Northumberland County, Virginia Deed and Will Book, 1655–1658

Northumberland County, Virginia Deed and Will Book, 1662–1666

Northumberland County, Virginia Deed and Will Book, 1666–1670

Northumberland County, Virginia Deed and Will Book, 1670–1672 and 1706–1711

Northumberland County, Virginia Deed and Will Book, 1711–1712

Northumberland County, Virginia Order Book, 1652–1657

Northumberland County, Virginia Order Book, 1657–1661

Northumberland County, Virginia Order Book, 1665–1669

Northumberland County, Virginia Order Book, 1669–1673

Northumberland County, Virginia Order Book, 1680–1683

Northumberland County, Virginia Order Book, 1683–1686

Northumberland County, Virginia Order Book, 1699–1700

Northumberland County, Virginia Order Book, 1700–1702

Northumberland County, Virginia Order Book, 1702–1704

Orange County, Virginia Deeds, 1743–1759

Orange County, Virginia Order Book Abstracts, 1747–1748

Orange County, Virginia Order Book Abstracts, 1752–1753

Petersburg City, Virginia Hustings Court Deed Book Abstracts, 1784–1787

Petersburg City, Virginia Hustings Court Deed Book Abstracts, 1787–1790

Petersburg City, Virginia Hustings Court Deed Book Abstracts, 1790–1793

Prince William County, Virginia Deed Book Abstracts, 1749–1752

Prince William County, Virginia Order Book Abstracts, 1752–1753

Prince William County, Virginia Order Book Abstracts, 1753–1757

(Old) Rappahannock County, Virginia Deed and Will Book Abstracts, 1656–1662

(Old) Rappahannock County, Virginia Deed and Will Book Abstracts, 1662–1665

(Old) Rappahannock County, Virginia Deed and Will Book Abstracts, 1663–1668

(Old) Rappahannock County, Virginia Deed and Will Book Abstracts, 1665–1677

(Old) Rappahannock County, Virginia Deed and Will Book Abstracts, 1668–1670

(Old) Rappahannock County, Virginia Deed and Will Book Abstracts, 1670–1672

(Old) Rappahannock County, Virginia Deed and Will Book Abstracts, 1672–1673/4

(Old) Rappahannock County, Virginia Deed and Will Book Abstracts, 1673/4–1676

(Old) Rappahannock County, Virginia Deed and Will Book Abstracts, 1677–1678/9

(Old) Rappahannock County, Virginia Deed and Will Book Abstracts, 1678/9–1682

(Old) Rappahannock County, Virginia Deed and Will Book Abstracts, 1682–1686

(Old) Rappahannock County, Virginia Deed and Will Book Abstracts, 1686–1688

(Old) Rappahannock County, Virginia Deed and Will Book Abstracts, 1688–1692

(Old) Rappahannock County, Virginia Order Book Abstracts, 1683–1685

(Old) Rappahannock County, Virginia Order Book Abstracts, 1689–1692

(Old) Rappahannock County, Virginia Will Book Abstracts, 1682–1687

Richmond County, Virginia Deed Book Abstracts, 1692–1695

Richmond County, Virginia Deed Book Abstracts, 1695–1701

Richmond County, Virginia Deed Book Abstracts, 1701–1704

Richmond County, Virginia Deed Book Abstracts, 1705–1708

Richmond County, Virginia Deed Book Abstracts, 1708–1711

Richmond County, Virginia Deed Book Abstracts, 1711–1714

Richmond County, Virginia Deed Book Abstracts, 1715–1718

Richmond County, Virginia Deed Book Abstracts, 1718–1719

Richmond County, Virginia Deed Book Abstracts, 1719–1721

Richmond County, Virginia Deed Book Abstracts, 1721–1725

Richmond County, Virginia Order Book Abstracts, 1694–1697

Richmond County, Virginia Order Book Abstracts, 1697–1699

Richmond County, Virginia Order Book abstracts, 1699–1701

Richmond County, Virginia Order Book Abstracts, 1714–1715

Richmond County, Virginia Order Book Abstracts, 1719–1721

Richmond County, Virginia Order Book, 1692–1694

Richmond County, Virginia Order Book, 1702–1704

Richmond County, Virginia Order Book, 1717–1718

Richmond County, Virginia Order Book, 1718–1719

Spotsylvania County, Virginia Deed Book, 1722–1725

Spotsylvania County, Virginia Deed Book, 1725–1728

Spotsylvania County, Virginia Deed Book: 1730–1731

Spotsylvania County, Virginia Order Book Abstracts, 1742–1744

Spotsylvania County, Virginia Order Book Abstracts, 1744–1746

Stafford County, Virginia Deed and Will Book, 1686–1689

Stafford County, Virginia Deed and Will Book, 1689–1693

Stafford County, Virginia Deed and Will Book, 1699–1709

Stafford County, Virginia Deed and Will Book, 1780–1786, and Scheme Book Orders, 1790–1793

Stafford County, Virginia Deed Book, 1722–1728 and 1755–1765

Stafford County, Virginia Order Book, 1664–1668 and 1689–1690

Stafford County, Virginia Order Book, 1691–1692

Stafford County, Virginia Order Book, 1692–1693

Stafford County, Virginia Will Book, 1729–1748

Stafford County, Virginia Will Book, 1748–1767

Westmoreland County, Virginia Deed and Will Abstracts, 1723–1726

Westmoreland County, Virginia Deed and Will Abstracts, 1726–1729

Westmoreland County, Virginia Deed and Will Abstracts, 1729–1732

Westmoreland County, Virginia Deed and Will Abstracts, 1732–1734

Westmoreland County, Virginia Deed and Will Abstracts, 1734–1736

Westmoreland County, Virginia Deed and Will Abstracts, 1736–1740

Westmoreland County, Virginia Deed and Will Abstracts, 1740–1742

Westmoreland County, Virginia Deed and Will Abstracts, 1742–1745

Westmoreland County, Virginia Deed and Will Abstracts, 1745–1747

Westmoreland County, Virginia Deed and Will Abstracts, 1747–1748

Westmoreland County, Virginia Deed and Will Abstracts, 1749–1751

Westmoreland County, Virginia Deed and Will Abstracts, 1751–1754

Westmoreland County, Virginia Deed and Will Abstracts, 1754–1756

Westmoreland County, Virginia Order Book, 1705–1707

Westmoreland County, Virginia Order Book, 1707–1709

Westmoreland County, Virginia Order Book, 1709–1712

www.ingramcontent.com/pod-product-compliance
Lightning Source LLC
Chambersburg PA
CBHW080337270326
41927CB00014B/3265

9781680345537